T0196128

A PARENT'S LOG

JAMES L. MARKS

authorHOUSE®

AuthorHouse™
1663 Liberty Drive
Bloomington, IN 47403
www.authorhouse.com
Phone: 1 (800) 839-8640

Published by AuthorHouse   02/17/2017

ISBN: 978-1-5246-7246-1 (sc)
ISBN: 978-1-5246-7244-7 (hc)
ISBN: 978-1-5246-7245-4 (e)

Library of Congress Control Number: 2017902530

Print information available on the last page.

PREFACE & DEDICATION

Ancient mariners were a courageous lot. They braved weather, unpredictable beyond the sum of their collective experiences and memories. They sailed into uncharted waters risking their lives and the fortunes of their vessels' owners against their ability to outguess reefs and fickle winds. They sailed in wooden ships that were fragile, absurdly small, and cruelly inconvenient. The hulls of these ships were susceptible to rot and decay caused by both aging and attacks of aquatic life forms.

Their navigational instruments, their maps and charts, were primitive beyond belief. Not until the invention of chronometers a few hundred years ago did they have any means of determining longitude beyond dead reckoning. They had no satellite communications systems, no LORAN or Global Positioning Satellite locators to compute their positions to within a few meters. They sailed on Spartan rations, for this was long before the days of refrigeration, vacuum sealers, and modern canning techniques.

Against these conditions they pitted their strength, endurance, skill, and their cunning. They fought merchants, pirates, and the sea. Sometimes they lost. But they learned from their mistakes (if they survived) and from the mistakes of their fellow sailors. They traded information. They improved their maps. They kept logs and rutters.

Today's sea travel must seem devoid of adventure to the ghosts of those ancient seamen. Computer databases make available at the touch of a keyboard button the location, depth, size, and color of virtually every rock on the planet. In case of computer crash, radar and sonar warn sailors of today's steel-hulled behemoths of icebergs, shoals, and other ships long before the lookouts of yesteryear could have spotted them from the crow's nests of the old clippers and galleons. With weather forecasting science able to predict the direction and velocity of wind to within five miles an hour three days in advance, and rain and snowfall to within a teacup or the capacity of a single three-horsepower snow blower, the dangers of sailing are reduced almost to the point of non-existence. Still, ships sink. They run aground. They collide with other ships, and with bridge abutments. They spring leaks far from maintenance docks. Occasionally they are still pirated.

Parenting is not unlike a sea voyage. We who embark on this voyage usually have at least a vague idea of our intended destination. We have (please, God!) carefully selected our ship's first mate; we have navigational aids undreamed of even a few decades ago. We have figurative provisions, and methods of preserving them that negate threat of pellagra, scurvy, rickets, and even the consuming of eating unsweetened limes. So with all these advantages, there is no excuse for parental shipwreck, right?

Then why are numbers for teenage alcoholism, juvenile delinquency, drug abuse, unwed pregnancy, STDs, and suicide higher today than they have ever been? Could it be that too many pilots have not even viewed the navigational manuals?--that too many craft owners have assumed that merely having acquired the designation of captain (parent) equips them with the skill and knowledge required to bring the ship safely to port? Whatever the reasons, parenting shipwrecks occur far too often. We are reminded of the adage: "Having a child no more *qualifies* a person to be a *parent* than possessing a *piano* qualifies one to be a *pianist*."

This book has been a long time in gestation. Material and ideas for it have been collecting for at least 50 of my 70-plus years. The acquisition of 8 children between 1972 and 1984 gave me ample reason to be concerned about the reefs, pirates, and storms that threatened my voyage. We were most fortunate. We've managed to avoid the reefs, fend off a pirate or two here and there, and weathered a few storms with only minor damage and perhaps a little seasickness. I've enjoyed the voyage.

Credit for this goes to the finest Mate, navigator, cook, and morale officer any sailor ever sailed with. She has kept me in touch with the Weather Bureau, and has kept me aware of the need to watch Radar Screens. And of course, it hasn't hurt that she has managed to put together the finest crew afloat.

To my mate (First, last, and always!) Renee, and to the crew; Loren, Heidi, Holly, Jamie, Jeremy, Jill, Jacki, and Doris, I dedicate these ramblings.

And to all who share my dread of shipwreck--GOOD SAILING!

PARENTAL PRIORITIES

Some years ago a teacher at our local high school approached me following the end-of-the-year awards assembly. Three of our children had received recognition (19 times!) for academic, musical, and athletic excellence. The teacher commented that he had noticed that certain surnames had a way of being repeated on these occasions, and that it would be a good idea for the parents bearing those names to pool their wisdom, and stage some sort of parenting clinic. I mentioned this exchange to John Cortell, a man whose children had also established impressive performance records athletically, academically, and socially. His response was, "Be honest with them, and no baby sitters," accompanied by a motion of his hand, shoulder high and parallel to the ground indicating, "End of comment."

I said, "Isn't that a little simplistic?"

He replied, "Not really. Make out your list of Do's and Don't's and run it across mine, and you'll probably find that every one of yours will be covered by one or both of mine." If he was mistaken, it was not by very much. He did elaborate a little. "I'm not saying a man should never take his wife out to dinner 'sans kiddies,' or to a movie once in awhile. But we didn't take any week-long excursions--or even any week-enders away while the kids were growing up. If we couldn't take them, we didn't go."

His concluding comment is worthy not only of repeating, but committing to memory. *"If your child ever gets the idea into his head that there is something more important to you than he is, then you have no right to be surprised when something becomes more important to the child than doing what pleases you."*

The performance of our children has been pleasing us for many years, and the recognition they have received for their efforts has been gratifying. And while we've never believed that our children were inherently any *brighter* than their classmates, it became abundantly obvious that *something* was different. Could it be that John Cortell's principle was being manifested here without our having articulated it?

We all have priorities in our lives, and one of the wonderful results of this is the incredible diversity of occupations, hobbies, and life styles of our citizens. What a boring world this would be if everyone chose to be farmers, or only wanted to steelhead fish in their spare time, or all wanted to drive 4-wheel drive pick-ups! Variety is not only the spice of life; it is a necessity if we don't want to die of boredom.

Still, there *are* concepts, principles, and priorities, universal acceptance and practice of which would make all of our lives more satisfying. Can anyone doubt that this world would be a better place if all of us obeyed the speed limits, or refrained from holding up gas station attendants and convenience store clerks?

Or if all of our children felt loved and appreciated?

FACTORS IN SUCCESSFUL VOYAGES

A study of nautical history will show that hazards of early sea travel were many and mighty. So many factors determined the success or failure of each voyage! The sea-worthiness of the craft--is the hull sound? Has anyone checked the weather report? Are the sails and rigging ship-shape? How about the instruments, charts, and maps? And crew skills--does anyone in the crew know how to tack against the wind?

Besides purely mechanical factors, where are we headed? Why? What is the cargo? Many an early trading ship made its intended landfall to find no market for its goods, or to find hostile natives, or pirates in ambush.

A thought-provoking verse relating to sea travel comes to mind:

> Mistakes have value, we have found
> Tho' true, some more than others.
> Not every sailor India bound
> America discovers.

Would that all errors committed on the voyage of Parenthood proved as fortunate as that of Columbus. Columbus died still believing he had found India. They benefited who recognized the magnitude of his error, and then exploited it. The error of assuming he was half-way around the world from where he actually was, was not repeated.

You who would sail the waters of Parenthood--inspect your vessels. Learn seamanship. Stay alert at the helm. Check your bearings often. Choose your mate wisely. *Choose your mate wisely.* CHOOSE YOUR MATE

WISELY! **CHOOSE YOUR MATE WISELY!** And never, never bet your skills, and the hull of your craft against known reefs. They are all well marked--by marker buoys, by lighthouses, and by the wrecked and broken hulls of those who ignored or challenged them.

IMAGES OF LOVE

Countless volumes of poetry have been written in scores of languages. Of all topics, *love* is one of the most popular--probably because the concept of love represents a universal experience to mankind. Every person who has reached maturity--or even adolescence--has sought it, craved it, experienced it, anguished over the lack or loss of it, rejoiced at its reciprocation, and marveled at how it affects one's moods and perceptions.

When one is in love, and finds that love returned in kind, it seems that any crisis can be dealt with, and any pleasant experience is doubly appreciated. When a romance ends, whatever fruit one happens to be enjoying turns sour; the music one hears becomes noise and discord; the rose-colored glasses through which he views the world become cloudy, bespecked, and out of focus.

With poets and song writers spending so much creative energy generating metaphors to which the consuming public can relate, it makes sense to look at the imaging process, and evaluate how well (or how poorly) some poetical and lyrical efforts capture the essence of love.

When elephant jokes were in vogue some years ago, one often heard was, "How do you sculpt an elephant?" The answer was, "Get a marble slab and a chisel, and chip away everything that doesn't look like elephant." For this method to work, obviously the sculptor needs (besides some sculpting skill) some idea of what an elephant looks like.

The mountain of material on the subject of love gives us a sizable block to start with, and much to chip away that doesn't look like Love. Forming a representative image of love requires defining some terms, looking at some concepts and perceptions, and putting them into perspective.

Describing love presents the same sort of problem shared by the blind men in John Godfrey Saxe's poem,

"The Blind Men and the Elephant:"

It was six men of Indostan
To learning much inclined,
Who went to see the elephant
Though all of them were blind,
That each by observation
Might satisfy his mind.

The First approached the Elephant
And, happening to fall
Against his broad and sturdy side,
At once began to bawl:
"God bless me, but the elephant
Is very like a wall!"

The Second, feeling the tusk,
Cried, "Ho! What have we here
So very round and smooth and sharp?
To me 'tis very clear
This wonder of an elephant
Is very like a spear!"

The Third approached the animal
And, happening to take
The squirming trunk within his hands,
Thus boldly up he spake:
"I see," quoth he, "the elephant
Is very like a snake!"

The Fourth reached out an eager hand,
And felt about the knee:
"What most the wondrous beast is like

Is very plain," quoth he;
"'Tis clear enough the elephant
Is very like a tree!"

The Fifth, who chanced to touch the ear,
Said, "E'en the blindest man
Can tell what this resembles most;
Deny the fact who can:
This marvel of an elephant
Is very like a fan!"

The Sixth no sooner had begun
About the beast to grope
Than, seizing on the swinging tail
That fell within his scope,
"I see," quoth he, "the elephant
Is very like a rope!"

And so these men of Indostan
Disputed loud and long,
Each in his own opinion
Exceeding stiff and strong.
Though each was partly in the right,
They all were in the wrong!

The theme of blindness in love has often been alluded to, and this one has some practical application. Keenness of eyesight varies. Some people are color-blind, some see not at all, and some perceive only blurs and shadows. Rare, it seems is the person who sees love with 20/20 vision, lighted, complete in proportion and perspective, and magnificently displayed. Rarer still for such a one to take to the studio to create the artistic masterpiece that enlightens and edifies us all. Would that they could give us the appreciation that causes us to want such an art object for our own--and the ability and perseverance to create it.

Erich Fromme stated that the problem of love is not in *being* loved, but in acquiring the ability and willingness *to* love. He must have been loved; must have known the warmth, comfort, and sense of self-worth that are warp and woof of the fabric of love. The ability to love is a skill--an *art*--Fromme writes, that can be *developed*. But knowing that one *is* loved--having before one the example of genuine love--is a tremendous advantage to the person who would approach the sculpting of love seriously.

A common theme in love poetry is the *object* of love. Another recurring theme is listing the things one is willing to do to prove the sincerity of his love. Climbing the highest mountain, swimming the deepest ocean--no feat is too daunting, if only the one loved becomes convinced--and returns that love. Granted that only the hopelessly sentimental accept these lyrics at face value, there must be a fair amount of sympathy with these veins of thought, else they would not be so overworked and so well received. Perhaps we tolerate--even embrace--the morbid or saccharine pictures painted in these songs because we lack the perception, conviction, or even the interest to protest.

One of the most damning indictments on our times is the success the advertising industry has had in persuading us that the secret to happiness is to become beautiful. If we will just brush our teeth with this toothpaste, and wash away our body odor with this soap, or mask it with this deodorant, eat and drink these products, control our hair with this styling gel, and fight our acne with that skin-care product, we will be beautiful, and therefore lovable. We diet, we tan, we exercise, we read self-improvement books all in an effort to be respected, admired, and loved--as if feeding and currying an elephant, and polishing its tusks, and bathing away its smell will improve our ability to carve its likeness in a block of granite!

Physical beauty--how we admire it! How we crave it--for our lovers and ourselves! How glowingly lyricists describe it! How justifiable our infatuation with it! (Read: How justifiable *IS* our infatuation with it?) How many hearts are broken because it equates so poorly with the abiding nature, the petrified durability, and the ageless dignity of granite sculpture? Physical beauty fades, and the popular consensus of what constitutes it varies. So romance that germinates and takes root in an attraction to physical beauty and/or sex appeal is doubly endangered. There's nothing wrong with admiring beauty--as long as we realize that beauty is no more a *definitive* element of love than physical size is the exclusive characteristic of the elephant. Physical beauty is neither a *requirement* of love, nor is its depth or quality *proportionate* to it.

If love is not an *attraction to beauty*, what is it? If we can't rely on the balladeers to enlighten us, to whom can we turn? Is there an accurate depiction, representative to all of us, or are we all doomed to the fate of those blind men, secure and satisfied with the single, incomplete conclusion to which our individual perceptions limit us?

The images projected by songsters are often flawed by their lack of dimension and perspective. It takes a degree of skill to create even the illusion of depth in an oil painting limited to two measurements. The only dimensions usually employed by song writers are the beauty and sex appeal of the love-idol and the intensity of the heartache endured by the sufferer of unrequited love.

Seldom do they consider the "weightier matters" of love. These include (among other things) *commitmen*t--to noble principles, rather than to one's own gratification. Included is *duty*--to resulting children, not to keeping oneself and one's partner perpetually entertained. And there is *sacrifice*--of energy, sleep, and personal comfort, not of one's list of other lovers.

Failure in many romances comes from unrealistic expectations lovers bring to the relationship, which are in turn the result of propaganda--distorted images projected by musicians, novelists, and script writers. Too many of them have no understanding of the concept of love. That there are shades, degrees, and types of affection is granted. One says he loves to fish, another loves his music, another basketball. A teenager loves his car, his high-dollar basketball shoes, or her earrings. None of these affections equates with the love that motivates lyricists.

There have been writers who *have* understood love, and who have defined it for us, taught us of its importance, and shown us how to practice it. For their efforts they have been scorned, stoned, beheaded--even crucified. The Lord calls them prophets; the world calls them madmen, fanatics, and charlatans. What do *they* say about love?

Among other things, they tell us that God IS love. They tell us that life eternal is to know this God, and the Christ whom He sent--so it behooves those who desire that blessing to learn something *of* love. They say that greater love hath no man than he who lays down his life for his friends. They say, "If ye *love* me, keep my commandments."

It matters not at all the King James translators used the English word *love* for several different Greek words. *Agape, philos,* and *eros* denote divine love, brotherly love, and romantic love, for these are facets of the same gem, though they are not synonymous.

Love, whatever its object, reflects an *understanding*, an awareness that a unique relationship exists between the lover and the love object. It reflects acknowledged *duty* with regard to that relationship. This duty varies with the nature of the relationship, but the principle is constant. It involves willingness to invest one's person, one's personality, as well as commitment and energy to constantly strengthening and improving all aspects of the relationship. *If this awareness and commitment are <u>not</u> present, we may call the affection a fondness, an attraction, a weakness for, or even an addiction. We ought not call it love.*

One who "loves" his hobby, or her trousseau, or his lodge brothers, but whose posture is essentially, "What's in it for me?" is *not* demonstrating love. He or she exhibits a visceral desire for gratification. The needs of the other persons or causes are not considered. When this syndrome manifests itself in a romantic relationship, and especially in a marriage, the potential for trauma is incalculable.

The demands of marriage include, *literally*, the laying down of one's life. They require the *commitment* to earn a living, to perform domestic duties, and the provision of what this generation calls *parenting*. Dilute that, or have one or both partners adopt a, "me first" posture, and that ideal image of love quickly crumbles. The urges that attracted the partners to one another initially will not provide the adhesive to patch it up for very long. *Don't take my word for this. Look around the gallery at the shattered monuments of beauty's, chemistry's, and sexual desire's mutual inability to equate with love.*

The principle of cause and effect is every bit as critical in nurturing and sustaining love as it is any other phase of human endeavor. Let one or both partners retreat from obeying the rules--the *laws* that govern love--let them disregard obedience to love's laws --and dimension is lost. The sanctity of marriage is besmirched; children born to it are offended. The weight of that offense becomes a millstone around the necks of those responsible.

Jesus said, "If ye love me, keep my commandments." If you love your wife, your husband, your children, keep His commandments. *If there is anything on this Earth that you love, and desire to possess for the eternities, obey the laws that pertain to the retention of it.*

A great--but greatly ignored aspect of our commonly accepted image of love is the yardstick of <u>obedience</u> by which it is measured. It is not measured by the flow of hormones; not by the number of children; not even by the number of moments, years, and crises shared and endured together. However we perceive love, whomever or what-ever the object of it happens to be, the qualitative and quantitative nature of it can be measured by <u>obedience</u> <u>to</u> <u>the</u> <u>laws</u> <u>that</u> <u>govern</u> <u>it</u>.

May we all become more obedient, more submissive to divine will, more loving. Would we not then *be* more lovable? Here is the smile brightener, the deodorant, the cleansing soap, the spiritual food, and the blemish remover calculated to carve both the *self*-image and the *projected* image we are intended to have--one that accurately and fully depicts the beauty, the courage, the majesty, and the humble dignity of Love.

LETTERS TO MY DAUGHTER

September 5th, 1965
Hameln, Germany

Dear Daughter,

I was just wondering today what I could give you for your birthday. This may sound funny to you now, because when you read this, it will have been a number of years since I set it down. But they say expectant fathers do funny things sometimes, and that is what I am at this moment. An anticipating, hoping, planning father.

Right now I can't see far enough into the future to determine what you would like to receive as a gift. You may be too young for perfume, and you may be too old for dolls. There would be something of a problem even if I knew you right now, since girls can be hard to buy for.

However, I was thinking today that *buying* gifts for birthdays is paradoxical, in a way. Because of the traditions of our society, we give presents to people celebrating birthday anniversaries. This is even true of the parents of the celebrating person. Wouldn't it be more logical if the birthday person would make an effort to express his appreciation in some way to his mother for playing the lead role in birthday number one? At any rate, the gift I would present you is not to be bought.

Irrational promises are somehow disgusting to me. But however this appears to you, I would promise this day that when you are born, the first gift from me will be your mother, my wife. If you are tempted to think that that would not be a gift within my power to give, let me explain.

Thousands of babies are born into the world every day and (except for multiple births) each one has a different mother. Idealists make fools of themselves

12

by claiming that all people are born equal, but that claim is proven false at the moment of birth, for they are certainly not born with equal opportunities. Some children have mothers who did not want to conceive them. Some have mothers who are not married. Even among those born to married mothers, there is such a variety of circumstances under which they are born that only the blind would maintain that babies are born with equal rights, privileges, and opportunities.

There are countless mothers who care no more for the health of their babies than to ignore medical counsel and common sense by using tobacco, alcohol, or narcotics during their pregnancies. There are mothers who do not realize that babies are spirit children of God, to be cared for with love and appreciation. There are mothers who do not put the well-being of their God-given children above all in this life.

Your mother will not be such as these. I mentioned that I could not see far enough into the future to be able to tell if you would prefer perfume or dolls, tricycles or sweaters. But whether you are one year old or twenty-one, and whether your time is taken up tending teddy bears or my grandchildren, one thing you will always need is a mother who loves you and your sisters and brothers (provided the Lord will be so good to us) more than anything on Earth, including self.

You will need a mother to be nurse when your knees are skinned, cook when you are hungry, seamstress when your dress is torn, and teacher when you are curious. You will need a mother who will be able to show you through her example what good mothers do, so that you can someday do the same for your little girls. And you will need a mother who is so strong in her faith that secretly and openly she can strengthen your father when he is weak, calm him when he is angry, and forgive him when he momentarily forgets that she is his partner and God-given complement.

Dear Daughter, I cannot promise you a car for your eighteenth birthday, nor even a plaything for your fifth. But the Lord has blessed me with enough wisdom to know that you need the best mother in the world, and with the desire and patience to find her. And should I fail to find her, and settle for second best, no other gift I could ever give would be worth the first salty tear I would shed when I realized what I had done.

You have my promise, Dear Daughter, that your mother, my wife, will be the finest, purest, lovingest woman under the sun.

Your Dad

+ +

March 26th, 1971
Provo, Utah

Dear Daughter,

If you are allowed to watch, you must be as excited as I am. You must be anxious to make your entrance here, and I am just as anxious to welcome you.

It has been several years since I first felt the desire to record my thoughts for future sharing with you. They have been eventful and educational years, punctuated with disappointment and occasional despair. My own weaknesses were generally to blame, and I realize that only the prayers of those who love me helped me to make it as far as I have come.

A time or two you may have been a bit concerned when it looked as though I were going to settle for less than I promised you. My limited insight kept me from seeing the whole picture for a period, but my promise to you to find the best eventually woke me to the danger of the course I was taking.

There is a twist I had not considered, and though I appreciate irony, I do not find it amusing. I have found your mother—or more accurately, I have been led to her, and I have recognized her. But in approaching the issue of our mutual future as delicately as I know how, I was startled to hear her express concern that she was not prepared for me.

If you are allowed to watch me often, you know that although I am something of an egotist, I am aware of my faults, and am also aware that if either of us has reason to be concerned about the lack of preparedness of the other, it is she.

How do I convince her that she is better prepared for me than I am for her without driving her away? How do I explain that the words of my promise to you were not enough to spur me to the degree of readiness I expected of her? How can I expose my weaker self and still profess the strength she has a right to expect?

She must strengthen me when I am weak, I said. Maybe I can convince her that she has already given me what strength I can claim. She has been told that I love her. She should know that I have loved her for years in a real way, and that the feeling that has developed in my heart these last few weeks is destined to inspire me to whatever good I accomplish.

She has been a source of encouragement to me since before she knew of my existence, and what she has represented in the last month and a half has caused me to carefully inventory my life and to begin major housekeeping.

She is fine, Daughter, as I promised she would be. She is pure and loving. She wants the father of her children to honor his manhood as well as her womanhood, so how could she not encourage him? She wants him to have unshakable faith, so how could she not stand beside him?

I'm waiting to hear from her right now, and I'm a bit apprehensive. I have recorded for her benefit many of the thoughts that are going through my mind, and she is reading some of the literature that has affected how I feel about her, about you, and about us.

I am praying for patience and strength. I have been waiting a long time for her—for you, Dear Daughter. And the waiting will soon be over. I'll be seeing you soon.

Your Dad

x x

May 25th, 1971
Provo, Utah

Dear Daughter,

And now your mother has developed a willingness--more--a *desire* to be ours. Her arrival at this point was not easy for her, nor for me, but her evident satisfaction indicates that she feels it was worth the wait.

She loves me! It is a warm and humbling experience, and though it is a bit scary, I am enjoying it. I have often found lacking in my character and personality much of what I have always held to be lovable. So the idea has risen in my mind that perhaps her measure of that which is worthy of her love is deficient. And I don't believe that it is alone the semi-blindness of newly discovered love that causes me to dismiss that thought.

A partly facetious remark was make the other night by a speaker in church that men generally look for the woman they want to marry, and women look for the kind of man they can inspire to become the man they wanted to marry. I suspect this to be partly the excuse your mother uses to justify her love for me.

But whether or not--I can already see positive changes in my being that are a direct result of her influence on me, and I am so grateful for this. I don't want to fight the changes; I realize that they are long overdue.

Your mother and I are going to see her parents this weekend. It seems fitting somehow that it should be at the end of "Finals Week," I feel a degree of confidence in facing this test that I have not felt in the others I've faced thus far--perhaps because I've studied for this one. I've put in something like ten years gathering information directly applicable to this subject, and I have put in more than a little time reviewing my notes.

I hope it will only be a little while until you are ready to receive these letters. I also hope and pray that I will have adequately prepared for that time.

My cup runneth over.

Your Dad

* *

I stand on a bridge overlooking the harbor. Ships of all descriptions lie at anchor, preparing for voyages--to who knows where?

I, who would be a sailor on the sea of parenthood, reflect on the perils that await me, and on the treasures that may be mine.

I do not want to fail. It behooves me, then, to know something of seamanship, of navigation, of communication, and of the histories of successful sailors.

I realize with both fear and excitement that there is much more to ensuring a successful voyage than booking my passage and stowing my gear. For here, of all departure points, he who fails to prepare, prepares to fail.

ROCKS IN THE HARBOR

Besides the hazards one faces on the open seas of parenthood, there are rocks and shoals that can threaten a vessel's safety before it leaves the harbor. Those who have not yet embarked--those who have not yet booked passage--would do well to take note of the channel markers.

Babies cost money. They may, even with what is termed "minor" complications, cost a *lot* of money. With no maternity insurance, and/or limited income, this voyage may not be right for you at this point in time. Starting out the first years of marriage and parenthood with heavy debts--medical or any other kind--may cause you to "bottom out" before clearing the harbor. If you are not married, you should strongly consider giving the ticket you've purchased to others better prepared to sail. Odds of successfully completing your voyage are overwhelmingly against you.

Why have you booked this passage? If you are becoming a parent to satisfy your mother's desire for grandchildren (and some have had no better reason), or because you envy your friend whose baby is so cute--or simply because you were just so attracted to that guy or girl you just couldn't wait for ideal sailing conditions, embarking under these conditions is almost certain to end in disaster.

* *

LETTER TO MY WIFE

Mother's Day, 1980

Sweet My Love,

In nearly 9 years of marriage I don't recall ever having taken time to inventory all the things I appreciate about you. I have tried to express on various occasions love and appreciation for incidental things that were noteworthy at the moment, and deserving of something more than the standard smile and thank you. It seems appropriate to list some of the things I may never have mentioned, and not necessarily because any single item may have been omitted, but because the cumulative effect that these things have had on me as I glance over the list is an increased awareness of what a special person you really are.

When did I *first* begin to comprehend the nature of my debt to you?

Was it the time I calculated for the sake of our son (who was feeling abused for being expected to wash a few supper dishes) that in the 7-plus years of his life you had already washed his dishes 7,000 plus times without once having murmured? No, that happened only a few months ago, and surely I have been aware longer than that.

Was it somewhere among the countless instances of people coming to me with reports of your secret little kindnesses, praising your virtues and sweetness? No, it had to be before any of those episodes, since I had been aware of similar deeds for some time.

I have pointed out to our children on several occasions that you have been laund-ress, housecleaner, bed maker, seamstress, nurse, teacher, playmate, disciplinarian, cook, and friend among other things, but I realize that those services could have been purchased from various agencies that would never have produced the end result that your caring and giving have generated. I am flattered when I am complimented on the appearance and decorum of the children, but I know that is *you* to whom the credit is due.

I realize that when I ask the children (even when they still have tears in their eyes from their most recent spanking), "Hey, who's got the greatest Mom in the world?" and hear their happy voices shout in unison, "We do!"

I appreciated the *first* time you went back on your promise not to waste money on a birthday or Father's Day gift and didn't kill me for stumbling onto it before the surprise was due. And every time since then.

When I look at our kids and reflect on the number of times you have literally laid your life on the line in the expression of love that brings them into the world, I marvel again at Mother's Love.

The list mushrooms. Add to it the times I came home to find the garden plowed, the plumbing in the extra bathroom repaired, and the times you have prayed us through stalled cars, money shortages, and medical complaints. And the time before we were married when the rent for our bridal apartment mysteriously appeared in the glove box of my car.

Whatever it is about you that causes $100 bills to appear anonymously in the mail just when they are most needed shows that my evaluation of your virtues is not overdone. No, others appreciate you too, for special reasons of their own.

My appreciation for you is not a recent acquisition. It goes back to before you showed the ability to keep me out of small claims court despite the fact that my income was often insufficient to cover the bills; to before you asked my pardon for crying out in the delivery room and making what you said was a fool of yourself; before it became a habit for me to *expect* to find little treasures in unexpected places...

Back to those precious months before our firstborn arrived; expecting them to be miserable (pregnant women are hard to get along with, I had been advised) and noting with delight that your otherwise sweet disposition never wavered. Even before that, before the month we discovered we were going to have a child, when you realized that I'm not always as clean shaven as I was on our Friday night dates.

Can my appreciation go any further back? Can it go back to the days of military service when living in close quarters with dozens of uncouth and inconsiderate men made me hope and know that someday I would have a roommate who understood rules of common courtesy? Or even back to college days, when confined life with companions selected for me by someone else encouraged me to hope that the day would come when I would have one like you to share my quarters with?

Can it go back any further? What is eternal marriage, after all? I don't know. I only know that if our marriage cannot exist eternally, I don't care whether I do or not. I can imagine no Heaven without it, and with, it even Hell would be tolerable.

Your Loving Husband

STRENGTH & DURABILITY
OF COMMITMENT

It has been noted that for the concept and institution of the family to endure, the human sex drive needs to be first strong, and second, more or less constant. If it weren't strong, most women would not be willing to endure the pain and discomfiture of child-birth more than once. If it were not more or less constant, few men would be willing to accept the responsibility of supporting a wife and the children that follow as a result of their sexual expression.

In evaluating the strengths and weaknesses of my own marriage, it occurs to me that while strength of sex drive is a factor in the duration of this union, this is not the *primary* cause for its quality and visible success. Strength and duration of other qualities and desires come into play, and it is with some humility and more shame I acknowledge that the degree of *commitment* from my wife exceeds mine by a wide margin.

I've changed diapers, but for every one I've changed, my wife has changed dozens--maybe hundreds. I've done dishes, but again, for every one I've done, she's done a mountain. I've driven kids to music lessons, ball games, concerts and parties, but again...I've made chili, soups, and meatloaves; she's fixed scores of meals to my one. I could run the list of standard parental services to pages and it is unlikely that there would be a single item where my contribution would be more than a few percentage points of hers. To put the depth of her commitment into perspective, I don't remember *ever* hearing her grouse about doing for her kids. I'm talking about (at this writing) 40-plus years of motherhood.

Besides doing for her children, she does for me. She pays the bills, shops, launders, and for years worked 8 hours a day to support my video club membership and Big Mac craving. I make sporadic and feeble attempts to express appreciation for all she does, and she generally accuses me of putting her on a pedestal. Ever the pragmatist, when I sent 15 roses and 8 carnations to her for our 15th anniversary, she chided me for extravagance.

In today's society, when many women her age have tried two or three different husbands, she stayed with her first. While many women either have their tubes tied or ordered their husbands vasectomized after their second deliveries, she continued to endure the discomfort, the inconvenience, and the unspeakable joy of bringing them into the world. And she can't see that she has done anything extraordinary.

In my rational moments, and when I examine my heart of hearts, complete with the weaknesses that qualify me for the appellation "natural man," I realize that the depth of her commitment is not based on her admiration for *me*. Her commitment to *principle*, and to the *institution* of marriage itself, was in force before she ever consented to become my wife, bookkeeper, laundress, cook, and the mother of 8 children.

The main reason for the ever-increasing numbers of failed marriages, failed parental efforts, failed businesses and careers, and failed friendships is, for the most part, *failure to commit to the principles on which the success of such enterprises depend.* Promises based on infatuation with beauty, artistry, sex appeal, or wealth are chancy because these are transient qualities and concepts. Commitment to parenthood--to chastity--to honesty--to charity--this is the stuff of which saints are made. And quality wives.

LEADING OFF

Achieving success in any enterprise is an uncertain thing. Many variables come into play--ability, training, commitment, politics, and occasionally, pure chance. Not the least of these variables is how we define success in the first place.

Experts from many disciplines have buried us in books providing surefire guidelines for the success we covet. *Think and Grow Rich, How to Win Friends and Influence People, Refine Your Golf Game*--the list is endless. We can improve our performance in any endeavor by implementing the transferable principles hawked by experts.

Where is the authoritative manual on successful parenting? Books on the subject abound, most of them written by university trained "behavioral scientists." The generation raised on the theories of Dr. Spock leads any in history in developmental dysfunction. Teen pregnancies, STD's, drug addiction, and suicides--what went wrong? Were the "how-to's" not followed? Or were the standards and banners of parental success mislabeled--or perhaps run up the wrong flagpoles?

A noted church leader of recent decades said, "No success can compensate for failure in the home." *Successful* parents produce children who, upon leaving the nest, are equipped to function in the adult world; who acknowledge and obey the laws of the land, of common sense, and decency. They respect the rights and sensitivities of others. They understand and accept that neither society, nor any member of it, *owes* them anything until they have *earned* it.

Bringing children to this point is neither a matter of pure chance, nor of politics. It is an enterprise that depends on observation, discriminatory selection, and application of universal truths. It requires commitment, concentration, and attention to detail.

Compare parenting to competing for major league baseball's batting champion-ship. Consider: By the time a rookie makes a big league roster, he has hundreds of sandlot and little league games behind him as both player and spectator. He has learned much by observation. He knows about commitment, or he'd never have made it this far. What will separate him from his teammates and opponents from this point on will be his ability to concentrate and focus.

Ted Williams, the last major leaguer to hit .400 in a season, watched every pitch the opposing pitchers threw. He catalogued speed, pitch selection, give-away motions--anything that would give him an edge. He selected his bats meticulously for weight, length, thickness, and proportion. Only twice in his career did he deliberately swing at pitches outside the strike zone--both of them went for home runs. He swung if, and only if, his chances of putting the ball into play were high. He exercised his hands, wrists, and arms until he could stop his home-run swing at any point in its arc. When he stepped to the plate, he *expected* to succeed.

How many arrive at the "plate" of parenthood so prepared and so focused? Too many have not even made a methodical selection of a partner--as if parenthood were some sort of inconsequential sandlot game, with only one bat to choose from. Too many take the first one available and step to the plate to take their cuts. Suddenly the ball is in play, and they don't even know the way to first base. Such players may get a hit or two in the parenting league, but they will never be contenders for MVP. I rephrase: Having a child no more qualifies one to be a parent than holding a bat qualifies him to hit home runs. Big league success in parenting (or any other endeavor) involves methodical, goal-oriented preparation. It involves knowing the rules of the game, pitch anticipation and selection, and the relative merits of high- and low-percentage play strategies. It involves knowing and respecting the limits of the strike zone. *And it involves mate selection.*

There will be times when a batting champion will not reach base. But at the season's end he'll not be remembered for the outs he made if he leads the league in runs batted in. But batting crowns aside--approval of the world aside--if his children know that he did all in his power to advance them to scoring position (read: prepare them for adulthood), he qualifies as a Most Valuable Parent.

ON HABITS & PATTERNS

Evidence shows that the way people are taught and treated as children will affect the way they think and function as adults. Criminologists can describe with amazing accuracy the backgrounds of serial killers or rapists by analyzing the nature of their crimes, victim selection, and other particulars.

How unfortunate that the ability to describe the background of a criminal from the clues he leaves does not extend to prescribing remedial or rehabilitative techniques. Aberrant behavior uncorrected until the subject reaches adulthood will generally continue unchanged until he is removed from the environment in which he commits his acts.

"Correctional Science," as applied to adult behavior, is an oxymoron. There have been prisons in the world for centuries. Studies show that regardless of the program used in penal facilities, success at changing behavior of adult habitual offenders is minimal.

Sixty-plus years of observing people have convinced me than habitual *anythings*-- smokers, drinkers, liars--church-goers, journal-keepers, or punctual employees--are not likely to change their behavior either--except of their own free will.

Our folk-lore reflects this. "As the twig is bent, so grows the tree." Another adage says, "You can't teach an old dog new tricks." On the positive side of this truism, one of Solomon's proverbs suggests, "Train up a child in the way he should go, and when he is old he will not depart from it."

The quality of the product in any human endeavor is determined by the quality and quantity of effort invested in it. Of course, a farmer may do all the right things with his wheat crop, and in the proper sequence, only to have his fields laid waste by a hail-storm or a plague of locusts, but *success favors the conscientious in any endeavor.*

Children who become happy and productive adults who contribute positively to society--are seldom the results of blind chance. Those who are taught early to answer for their own acts; who are taught to think creatively; to be responsible for specific assignments; to create their own wholesome and acceptable entertainment; to experience satisfaction in jobs well done--tend to continue these patterns long after leaving the nest.

Those who desire for their children fulfillment at the adult level will see to it *personally* that their "twigs" are bent in the right direction. They will not depend on pasture grazing to put desired "beef" on their calf crop. They will corn feed them daily, and care for them as though each was intended to be Grand Champion at next year's fair.

They do not leave introduction to reading instruction to Bert, Ernie, and Big Bird. They don't leave their moral and religious training to television evangelists, or even to their own clergyman--they see to these things themselves.

Such parents know, while standing in the "on deck" circle what they want their children to be able to do 18 or 20 years down the road. They understand that the time to teach batting fundamentals is long before their child finds himself at the plate in a key game, bottom of the 9th inning, bases loaded, 2 out, and behind 3 to zero on the scoreboard, and 0 and 2 in the count.

GOALS & HOPES

There are countless courses to help people succeed at various undertakings. Learn to Drive, Learn to Sell, How to Lose Weight, How to Gain Weight, How to Re-distribute Weight. Enrollees succeed or fail for the most part in proportion to their *commitment to the goal* implied in the course title.

Success at raising children is less a matter of blind luck than many suppose. Much of it is determined by which (or whether) goals were established at the outset. We assume that every parent shares some hopes and dreams for his or her children that are similar to ours. We do not presume to decide for other parents *what* goals they ought to establish for themselves or their children with regard to either performance levels or numbers. We are keenly aware that there are many (perhaps even more) successful parents who have knowledge on this subject worth sharing.

Having clearly defined goals in any undertaking makes its realization simpler, since outlining the steps necessary to achieve them is reduced to a mechanical process. We had some goals and hopes when we got into the parent game--some fairly specific, some vague.

Following is a list of hopes we had for ours, not intended to be all-inclusive, and not necessarily prioritized. We wanted for them:

1. To be able to function in the artificially competitive atmosphere of the classroom.
2. To know how to be a **F**riend, and how to choose Friends wisely.
3. To respect the property, space, and sensitivities of others.
4. To understand the *cost* of things, the *value* of things, and that sometimes these have little to do with one another.

5. To know that their parents love them, and that though we may not always agree on particulars, we both want what is truly best for them.

6. To take themselves seriously, but to realize that it is not necessary to always be serious.

7. To believe that any goal they set for themselves is attainable, and that it is not necessarily a cop-out to *change* one's goals when new opportunities or new data present themselves.

8. For them to leave home (when the proper time arrives) with both *roots* and *wings*.

9. To know that happiness and success do not have to be measured by income, nor by the accumulation of toys.

10. To know that nothing of *lasting* value will ever come to them by any other means than their own efforts. Nothing, that is, except our love for them.

11. To know that whatever our goals, whatever theirs, and whatever methods used to accomplish them, we are all ultimately answerable to our Creator first, ourselves second, and our critics and self-appointed judges not at all.

FRIENDS & ACQUAINTANCES

Everyone needs friends, and everyone with many years behind him has anguished over friends poorly chosen. Caring parents need to be concerned about the friends and acquaintances of their children. Can we control, or even influence the selection? This will depend largely on what long-term goals we have selected for them.

As children grow out of the toddler stage they begin to make acquaintances outside the immediate family. These will be children of our friends, neighbors, pre-school mates, Sunday school mates, and eventually classmates in public or private schoolrooms. We have no control over some of these environments and only limited control over others, so it is almost certain that our children will have some association with those that we may find undesirable. How to deal with this?

Try to make your home a haven for kids. We had over-nighters for 25 years. We had after-schoolers, after-practicers, and after-dancers. The popcorn, pizza, and assorted leftovers that vanished out of our pantry and refrigerator during those years would probably have fed some third world nations. Cookies have been on the endangered species list since long before our first child reached kindergarten.

Toys cluttered our living room (not all of them left by our children), bicycles clogged our driveway (ditto), and not all the mud tracked through our kitchen came from feet we shod. Not all the milk drunk or spilled was due to the thirst or clumsiness of ours. Videos played far into many nights, entertaining ours and others. But that's okay.

When they were eating *our* leftovers, watching *our* videos, listening to *our* kids' music, we knew where *ours* were, and who they were with. (In

Heidi's case, we knew *whom* they were with.) And we had some control over the entertainment selected, and the refreshments being served.

When ours went overnight with friends, they were reminded and admonished on proper behavior, and specifics were important. They knew to call us if for any reason they felt uncomfortable. We were called once when an illegal substance appeared, several times for sudden illnesses, and a time or two when a young one just got lonely for Mom.

When guest children were in our home, they were invited to join our program, which included (among other things) blessings on meals, kneeling prayers at bedtime, and other rituals we feel gave solidarity to our family. Interestingly, those who chose to join us (and none were compelled) tended to be the ones who returned, and not because we controlled the invitations. More than one commented that they thought these things were "cool," and wished they did them in their own families. It appeared that our children tended to bond more strongly with those who shared their values and priorities. This may not constitute *control*, but I suppose there was some *influence*. Now all 8 of ours have finished high school, and have scattered to the winds. But we still get returning guests from afar, visitors and phone calls (some collect) from Texas, letters from Georgia and Germany, and points in between, all from friends of our grown children who know those kids are thousands of miles from us.

They were welcome. They *are* welcome. They partook of our friendship, and they are Friends.

THE MESSAGE OF INCONSISTENCY

The prudent and caring parent understands and appreciates that *consistency* is a highly important part of successful child rearing. Rules, policies, and guidelines are spelled out, enacted, and enforced. Combinations of rewards and consequences are used to impress upon children that there are advantages and disadvantages to pursuing certain behaviors.

It is frustrating when efforts to instill proper behavior patterns are undermined--in some cases *undone*--by the irrationality and irresponsibility of others.

Some years ago our son went on an extended trip with his soon-to-be graduating high school class. Prior to departure some very specific rules were spelled out regarding the use of alcohol, complete with consequences for violation. Among these was denial of the privilege of marching with the graduating class for offenders who were caught.

A number *were* caught, and sentence was pronounced. There was much weeping and wailing, the pleas tending towards the defense, "We've worked 13 years for this--it's only a single offense--it's too harsh." The high school principal whose job it was to impose and carry out the sentence took a lot of heat.

I attended a meeting involving the young offenders and their parents. When I voiced my support of the policy and its enforcer, I was challenged by one of the students involved. I was told, "It's none of your business, Mr. Marks--your kid wasn't one of the ones caught, otherwise you'd probably be on our side."

I assured the student and everyone there that it *was* very much my business, whether or not my child was one was among the offenders. I told them, "I've been trying my best for almost 18 years to teach my kids that our acts have *consequences*. If we choose proper behavior, we can expect to be treated in certain ways. If we misbehave, we can expect quite different consequences. If my kid comes out of this experience having learned that, 'It doesn't matter whether I obey law or not, the result is the same,' I run the risk of seeing 18 years of my best effort go down the tube. I am not going to stand silently by and allow that to happen. You bet this is my business."

My position was not based on a dislike for the offenders. Several were friends of my children, and their parents were friends of mine. I realized then, and do now, that a single act of disobedience does not make a person irredeemably evil, or loathsome, or unworthy of our love and support. But it makes them *wrong*--and if we have their best interests at heart we will teach them that it is better to act properly the first time, when all that is on the line is some minor inconvenience and embarrassment. I told them further, "If at some later date the legal system finds it necessary to teach you acceptable parameters of alcohol use, it may involve the revocation of driving privileges, heavy fines, or even imprisonment. It could even involve the loss of innocent lives. Be thankful that someone loves you enough to teach this lesson *now* at such a nominal cost."

Allowing this lesson to wait until *dire* consequences must be dealt with is the not the technique of a loving parent. Sometimes duty does, in very deed, involve inflicting pain on those we love.

THE WORTH OF CHILDREN

My father was a timber faller, and he tended to see individual trees--and even entire forests--as potential homes, newspapers, and other wood products for the use and comfort of people, thus as income for him. As a salmon and steelhead fisherman, he interpreted factors such as weather, stage of the river, tides, and even the time of day in terms of fishing conditions. Professional soldiers may view terrain in terms of troop and weapon placement, defensibility, and fields of fire.

Biologists who study oxygen cycles see trees as oxygen producing organisms, essential to the perpetuation of life generally, and ecosystems particularly. Those who deal with fish in pet stores may view them as objects of beauty--even as art forms, as in fact some exotic species seem to be. Landscape architects and artists are likely to view terrain with eyes more sensitive to beauty than to military tactics.

The perceptions of loggers, fishermen, and soldiers are not *wrong*, nor are their assessments invalid. Nor are those of the biologists, aquarium dealers, or landscape architects. But they are constricted, and overlook the perceptions and values of others.

What about children? How do we perceive *them*? Are they means to personal ends, or are they ends in themselves? Do we see them as raw material--something solely to be used to our personal advantage? *However we view children, those views will be reflected in the methods we use to rear them.*

What if we view children as job security? Specifically, what if we view *miscreant* children as job security? What if it were to my advantage for children to require *my* counseling services before they could fit into society?

Would it make a difference in the tactics I would recommend to parents, whose job it is to give them that preparation?

There is in our society today a growing group of people who have taken for themselves the title, "Child Behavior Specialists," who have acquired degrees labeling them, "Masters of Behavioral Science." They have figuratively established foresting techniques, devised fishing strategies, and written manuals on terrain tactics as though all trees were evergreens, all fish were bass, and all terrain consisted of hills of the same slope and configuration. They generate textbooks based on the assumption that *all* children are equally receptive and responsive to the same stimuli; that mere disapproval on the part of a parent will cause *any* child to forsake forbidden behavior.

Much of their counsel is absurd; much of their focus is grossly misdirected; much of the data they use to justify their propaganda is distorted and irrelevant. Most disturb-ing, their motivation seems to be to corner the market on child rearing techniques. None of this would be alarming if the children their methods produce were demonstrably superior to children reared on other proven programs.

Children differ in temperament as bass differ from steelhead. Those who "angle" for quality children need to adapt their tackle and methods to the species desired. If you want children who, upon reaching adulthood, need the services of psychological counselors, it makes sense to rear them according to the dictates of such counselors. If you want your children to reach adulthood capable of making rational judgments; able to understand the consequences of improper behavior; willing to be responsible for their acts--then it makes sense to use tactics calculated to develop these skills. Children are individuals that respond to different tactics. "Catching" trophy specimens requires tackle and techniques selected with the goal in mind.

Someone has said, "All people are alike, and all people are different. Upon these two principles all human wisdom is based." All children need to be fed, clothed, housed, loved, appreciated, disciplined, loved, encouraged, *dis*couraged, loved, taught, challenged, and loved. They need to understand parameters of acceptable behavior. They need to learn that ignoring or willfully violating those parameters brings consequences.

Under unique and original (all people are different) we would list: Sensitivity to pain, embarrassment, and loss; desire to please, desire to spite, desire to avoid conflict. And let's toss in senses of humor, of justice, and shame; interests in the arts, hobbies, and other diversions.

These perceptions are based on my observation of *children*, not laboratory rats. They are based on the experience of watching and monitoring the progress of my own children as they have grown to adulthood. I've watched them deal with the traumas and dramas that go with achieving that state, and I've struggled with them as I changed lures, timing, and casting techniques. Methods that worked with some didn't work with others, so we found or developed different ones. Some methods *did* work with all of ours, though we'd be the last to insist that they will be equally effective with all of yours. Still, we encourage you not to dismiss them out of hand- -unless you disapprove of our finished products.

We viewed our children as gifts. We viewed ourselves as stewards with the awesome responsibility of teaching those children to learn to conduct their affairs according to the desires and purposes of their Creator, and by definition, to the advantage of themselves and mankind with whom they are obliged to share the planet.

We've chosen our parenting methods accordingly. We encourage all who enter the parenting enterprise to choose the methods they use from a framework of *desired finished product*, weighed against the success records of those whose methods they opt to follow. And remember Winston Churchill's maxim: "However beautiful the *strategy*, you should occasionally look at the *results*."

TECHNIQUES & SOURCES

People have been raising children on this planet for many centuries, and many techniques have been tried and tested with varying results. Predictably, much of what has been said contradicts our experiences, our sensibilities, and our outlooks.

I'm amused at a golfer friend of mine who subscribes to several monthly golfing publications. Every issue is filled with articles on how to hit golf balls. Given that each course--each *hole* on each course--has its own peculiarities, I ask, "How many different ways can there possibly be to hit golf balls?" Still, each month a dozen editors put together new magazines with new suggestions, new ideas, new philosophies, sometimes contradicting what has been said in previous publications! And make no mistake about it, this is not done for the ostensible purpose of helping you improve your golf game--it is done in the interests of selling magazines.

All the coaching, writing, all the clinics given, and all the clubhouse gab sessions are put into perspective by the observation of one successful (though highly unorthodox) golfer who, when criticized for the lack of fluidity of his form said, "The scorecard doesn't ask *how*, it asks *how many*."

The idea for these ramblings germinated with the recurring suggestion from friends that I write a book. These suggestions usually followed discussions of the performances of our children. The consensus seemed to be that if one wants children who perform and behave as ours, it makes sense to use the methods and techniques--the formula, if you will--that we used.

While this assumption is flattering, it leaves some questions unanswered. Are there different techniques that will produce similar results? Does the response of *our* children to these tactics guarantee that *yours* will respond the same way? And what if you as a parent *prefer* that your children behave differently?

The behavior of children is not an exact science, and the policy that universities have granting degrees naming people, "Masters of Behavioral Science" does not nullify that. One adolescent counselor was heard to comment, "I once had 5 theories on how to raise children. I now have 6 children--and NO theories." While said partly in jest, the quip contains an element of wisdom. Personalities of children (and of parents implementing parenting tactics) cause them to react unpredictably--inconsistently--to identical situations. Even the same child will respond differently at different times. Chalk it up to moods, hormones, peer pressure, or whatever.

Outcomes of interactions involving human personalities are less predictable than chemical reactions in lab experiments, or physics demonstrations involving inert bodies. The psychology classes I attended in college left me unconvinced that experiments conducted on laboratory rats yield much data that is transferable to human behavior.

In our attempts to generate specific behavior in our children *we have generally preferred to employ methods used by parents of children whose behavior we admire*. Some of the principles we used are at least as old as Solomon, who observed, "Train up a child in the way he should go, and when he is old he will not depart from it." Some are as contemporary as our own children, who have reminded me on several occasions that anger with oneself is not license to shriek at children.

Be open to suggestions, especially from parents whose children are well-behaved. Likewise, be cautious of textbook formulas, the data of which are often analyses of hypothetical situations, or even experiments performed on non-human subjects.

Lastly--if you have already raised your children, and are fortunate enough to be grandparents--and if you really feel that these musings contain information that might be applicable to your grandchildren-- please, *please*--believe that sending your daughter-in-law a copy of these ramblings with passages underlined (while flattering to us) is almost certain to generate feelings for which we are anxious to disclaim responsibility.

LOVE & COOKIES

Once upon a time there was a family of children who loved cookies. Being fairly normal children, they had their particular favorites. On the other hand, they were not fanatically selective. I mean, there are cookies, and there are *cookies*--and then there are Mom's made-in-the-oven chocolate chips and snickerdoodles.

Over the years their dad noticed some interesting behaviors developing. In the cupboard where the ingredients were stored you could usually find chocolate chips, vanilla, sugar, flour, cream of tartar, shortening, baking powder, cinnamon, and various other condiments available for use, depending on the day's recipe.

Some of these kids liked chocolate chips. Others were partial to sugar. Frequently recipes had to be substituted or amended because when it came time to mix ingredients, items believed by the cook to be in ample supply were gone. Now, even the chocolate-cheat and the sugar-snitch would admit that Mom's finished cookies were much tastier than the ingredients they were pilfering. But, well, one little handful would not matter (and perhaps a spoonful later tonight after everyone is asleep wouldn't either).

On baking days Mom would usually have to make two batches of cookie dough to produce a single batch of cookies, because one would vanish into a mysterious vacuum designed for the demise of cookie dough. Again, the kids would admit that *finished* cookies were better. But hey! Raw dough isn't bad--and it's available *now*, and not 20 minutes-in-the-oven and 10 minutes cooling later. Of course cookies weren't the only item on Mom's menu. There was bread--white, whole wheat, an occasional pie or two, and birthday cakes.

*

Marital bliss--Love--is not exclusively sex, any more than cookies are exclusively sugar. Certainly sugar is an important component of cookies. But it is only one, and is not necessarily the most important one. Any baked good is a combination of sugar, flour, yeast, shortening, and flavoring--taste each of these separately sometime! Yeast, alone, is awful; a teaspoon full of shortening will make you gag; a teaspoon of pure cinnamon will make your eyes water.

Marital bliss is a combination of bills, sex, humor, shared interests, unshared interests, bills, births, sickness, bills, meals, anniversaries, bills, prayers, outings, bills--things and services purchased through the paying of those bills--and many other things.

Marital bliss--and cookies--are *combinations* of the right ingredients, in the correct proportions, baked at the correct temperature, and for the proper duration. Don't ever trade a chance at the finished product for one of the ingredients.

TATTOOS & PARENTHOOD

When we opt to perform an act, we often have little choice as to the outcome or impact of that act. When we jump from a diving board, remaining dry is not an option--unless the pool is dry--in which case the consequences are more predictable and less favorable than either wetness OR dryness. And jumping blindfolded, and unaware of *whether* there is water in the pool or not, will not change the consequence one iota.

Many *decisions* are changeable. If we don't like a new hairdo, it will grow out. A poor choice on a car purchase can be traded in on a different one, with only some dollars lost. Careers can be changed, even to great advantage, so spending years after high school graduation as a mill worker, a farm hand, or soldier does not permanently condemn any-one to a life he finds to be unpleasant after the novelty wears off.

How many soldiers and sailors have sobered up after a week-end binge to find their arms or chests decorated by a grotesque tattoo, only to realize they are condemned to wear it for the remainder of their days, long after the approval of their buddies has faded into oblivion?

Of such lasting impact are decisions we make regarding the expression of our sexuality. Many have made the leap from the diving board of virginity believing that they could opt to remain dry, never considering the impact conceiving a child might have on their future options.

I once discussed with a co-worker the options that were now open to him. He had a child by a woman to whom he was not married. He was 23 years old, the mother 20. She had decided to enroll in college in a distant town to "better herself." In discussing her desires with this young father, she indicated a realization that she hadn't finished growing up yet, and needed some "space" to "find herself."

He agonized over the well-being of his child. The mother could not possibly give proper attention to her studies *and* a pre-toddler, nor could it even be hoped that she could find "suitable" day-care (whatever that is!) in a strange town, and even if she could, what of the cost? He felt he could do better where he was, with both his parents and hers willing to watch the child part of the day, and he would gladly give his off-duty hours providing all the support and care he could. She found this unacceptable. The child was HERS. With no marriage in force, what "rights" did he have?

On the one hand he was glad that with no marriage in force at least the division of property was a simpler matter. On the other hand, perhaps with a marriage contract he would have some legal claim to custody of the child. Any way you look at it, it was a traumatic and painful situation.

Parenthood is not an on-again-off-again proposition. It is not a leap from a diving board that will dry out in a few minutes on a summer afternoon, nor is it an unflattering hair-do that will grow out in a few months. It is more like a tattoo, since however oblivious to the future we were when we acquired it, however pleased or displeased we are with it after sobering up--we are stuck with it for life. There are, of course, methods of removing tattoos, but they are excruciatingly painful, and they leave scars.

The decision *to* express your sexuality is one thing; the *results* quite another--and those results *can* be permanent, painful, and debilitating. Any decision that may result in the "tattoo" of parenthood must be made soberly, carefully, with a view that sees farther down the road than the "morning after."

A CASE FOR CHASTITY

The trend of sex education in the public schools is a study in futility. The argument, "Kids need to know, and they aren't getting the information at home," was used to justify a curriculum designed to teach adolescents the Latin names for every organ, tissue, and fluid involved in human reproduction. Illustrations and working models of human genitalia have been introduced into mixed classrooms, and presentations have been given covering topics from menstrual cycles to orgasms, and from conception to abortion--all in a judgment-free environment. Heaven forbid that a public school teacher ever be guilty of imposing his or her concept of *morality* on our children!

The aim of this thrust was ostensibly to provide kids with enough information to make "intelligent choices" regarding their sexual conduct--as if *any* choice, the results of which can be as traumatic, as permanent, and as serious as those related to copulation--*can* be made intelligently without considering "rightness" or "wrongness"!

Since the advent of sex education in public schools, figures for teenage pregnancies and abortions, STDs, and suicides have skyrocketed. Providing education-- even when accompanied by free condoms--exacerbates, rather than alleviates the problem. Granted that the public schoolroom is not the proper forum for dispensing lectures focusing on the theme, "God said 'Thou shalt not...'"--can't a teacher justifiably condemn teenage promiscuity on purely pragmatic grounds?

Never in the history of the world has there been a generation of teenagers so inept that they have failed to figure out how to save the race from extinction. From many societies we have little written record of how much sex education was given to their children. But from most we do have records that indicate what they were taught in terms of citizenship, duty, honor, morality, and values.

The civilizations we admire, the religious figures we revere and whose legacies we treasure taught chastity, filial loyalty, and family solidarity. Conversely, those cited as negative examples are those that ceased to value chastity and the sanctity of marriage.

Teaching kids how to copulate without teaching them "rightness" or "wrongness" is as senseless as teaching them how to strike matches without mentioning that fires at improper times, or in improper places can be catastrophic. Knowing how to light a match is valuable information. But not knowing that there are times and places where lighting matches *must be avoided* at all costs is potentially fatal to both strikers of matches and everyone within miles of a powder magazines and gasoline pumps.

In civics we discuss pros and cons of Democratic and Republican platforms. In forensics we debate relative values of myriad ideas and developments. In P.E. class we discuss pros and cons of training regimens and diets. Why can't we do the same with sex education? If we can't say "sinful" or "righteous," can't we at least say "bad" or "good," or even "wise" or "unwise"?

Let's line up pros and cons of teenage sexual activity. Without having polled high school students specifically on their promiscuity, I guess that on the "pro" side we would have to list: (1) It feels good, (2) Everyone else does it, (3) I have to be sexually active to maintain my social status. It is hard to imagine any reason a teenager would use that wouldn't fall under one or the other of these headings.

Why abstain?

First--in fact, first through tenth is this: ***Teenagers are simply not equipped to deal with the possible results.***

What 15-year old girl is prepared--emotionally, intellectually, or physically (most are still growing) for pregnancy and motherhood? And remember that no condom, no spermicidal foam, no IUD, and no pill or calendar is 100% reliable. Granted that there is an alternative to out-of-wedlock births with abortion, what teenage girl should be willing to risk her future reproductive capabilities to infection or surgical incompetence? And if she opts to deliver the baby, is she prepared for the emotional anguish of giving it away? What 16-year old boy is emotionally equipped for fatherhood, or financially equipped to feed *himself*--much less his girlfriend and a baby?

But what if the boy or girl is sterile? However enjoyable sex is, AIDS is fatal. Syphilis and gonorrhea are painful, debilitating, embarrassing, and potentially fatal. And again, no condom is failsafe. *There is simply no such thing as safe sex.* And remember that for the purposes of AIDS--when you have sexual contact with a person, *you expose yourself to everyone with whom that person has previously had sexual contact.* And AIDS cannot be aborted.*

A point for guys to remember: Four inmates I know of in the prison where I worked for many years are in prison for killing men who had behaved improperly with the daughters or wives of those inmates. In more conservative areas of the country, these men would likely have never been indicted, much less convicted. But convicted or not, *their victims are just as dead.* Many fathers and husbands are so protective of their daughters and wives that incurring their wrath is as fatal as AIDS--and quicker.

Are you prepared to deal with that risk?

But beyond the *immediate* physical consequences of expressing your sexuality, consider the *future.* There will come a time when you will want to commit to someone that your sexual favors will be exclusively for them. A history of bed-hopping will negate your credibility. Who should believe that a person whose lovers number in double digits will ever be exclusive with his or her sexual favors?

Indiscriminately striking matches causes untold loss in lives and property. There are places and times for fires, and when they are kept in stoves, fireplaces, and boilers (where they belong), their benefit to mankind is immeasurable. But look at the aftermath of a forest fire. Besides the obvious *immediate* loss of timber and wildlife, erosion washes the topsoil into streams and rivers, killing fish and rendering hillsides barren of future productivity.

Likewise for human sexual expression. The heartache, sorrow, and pain--not to mention expense--of indiscriminate sexual activity have ruined whole civilizations, and are rapidly ruining ours. Exclusive, discriminate, responsible and proper expression of sexual desire is the pinnacle of human enjoyment. The consequences, when handled by mature, responsible, equipped adults, are among the ultimate in earthly delights.

If it isn't permissible to allow our teachers to say, "Teenage sex is naughty," let's *require* them to impress on our young people that it is a least very, very unwise, and that they are simply not equipped to deal with the consequences.

*(See appendix on page 185)

THINGS IN THEIR PROPER ORDER

Events in the adult world happen according to an agenda, a procedure, a recipe--some sort of predictable order. Some are so obvious that we don't even reflect on the order; it is automatic. Foundations forms are placed, used, and removed prior to walls being framed and raised. No carpenter needs to be reminded of this every time he begins construction. No potter would dream of firing his clay before molding it.

It is hard for teenagers to understand that much of their capacity for happiness as adults is determined by willingness to follow established schedules. Much of what they are *forbidden* to do, or even encouraged *not* to do, is not because the acts themselves are evil or dangerous. Often it is simply because *the time is not right.*

We worry about how early kids should begin dating. What about the use of make-up? And when can we leave them alone without supervision? The question in each instance is not *whether,* but *when.* Of all elements in the life of a growing human being, there is no other single activity, the timing of which has greater lasting impact than that of sexual expression.

Teenagers need to know that sexual activity prior to physical and emotional maturity, prior to independence from parents, prior to being both capable *of* and willing *to* make permanent commitments--is *wrong.*

It is wrong the way picking unripe fruit is wrong, or letting popcorn pop prior to putting the lid on the pan. You can't string a fence before the posts are sunk. You can't pass the line of scrimmage before the ball is snapped. These acts are against rules--of agriculture, culinary arts, ranching, and football. Premature sexual activity is against the laws of obligation to the forces of life within you.

There is no "safe" way to be sexually active, even if you are married to your partner, even if both are healthy and willing, and both equipped and willing to deal with pregnancy, delivery, and child rearing. There are risks built into the human reproductive process that go far beyond risks of being embarrassed or inconvenienced--*and teenagers are not equipped to deal with them*. These risks even include the risk of life.

Those who teach that it is "unrealistic" to instruct teenagers to abstain from sexual activity are wrong--even more wrong than the teen-agers who become sexually active. They are wrong the way coaches are wrong who encourage their players to use illegal blocks, or late hits, or illegal pitches. They are breaking the rules, and are guilty of abetting the young in breaking them. Penalties for these infractions are not measured 5 yards at a time, or by loss of downs, or free passes to first base. They are measured and paid in broken lives, unloved and uncared for babies, and injuries no trainer can tape up.

TEN COMMANDMENTS OF PARENTHOOD

I shy away from the "magic formula" approach to raising children, though clearly there are some techniques that I perceive to be more effective than others. It seems appropriate to set some of them down, and though we'll use a "Ten Commandments" format, we would prefer that they be seen in the context of George Orwell's 6 rules governing writing style--that is, to be relied on when instinct fails.

I. Thou shalt hold no other Project, Hobby, or Career to be more deserving of thy best effort than thy role as Parent.

II. Thou shalt not make idols, neither of thy activities nor thy children; thou shalt bow down to none of them; nevertheless thou shalt hold inviolate thy responsibility to instruct and to prepare thy children for responsible adulthood.

III. Thou shalt not speak in vain, neither *of* nor *to* thy children, but shalt reprove as needed, showing increased love thereafter.

IV. Remember thy time each day with thy children; keep it holy and wholesome. Beguile thee not in the belief that "quality time" on a monthly basis is any more redeeming for thy children than praying once a week is sufficient unto the cleansing of thine own soul.

V. Honor thy spouse, that the days in which thy children grow and develop may be filled with the comfort and security of the love of *both* parents.

VI. Thou shalt not kill nor weaken the respect and trust of thy children.

VII. Thou shalt not be unfaithful to the commitments and interests of thy children, nor let thine affection be drawn away from them by job, hobbies, or fatigue.

VIII. Thou shalt not steal from story time, bed time prayers, nor walks in the park or on the beach; nor from thy child's ballgames, spelling bees, and recitals.

IX. Thou shalt not bear false witness unto thy child, for children believe and trust thee, and the Lord and thy children shall hold him guilty who violates truth and trust.

X. Thou shalt not covet dollars and the goods dollars will buy above the love and respect *of* and thy responsibility *to* thy children.

John Cortell's maxim sums it up: "Be honest with them, and no baby sitters." He was right. These guidelines (and a dozen or more others I was tempted to include) all fit under one or the other or both of these ultimatums. And his summarizing justification for his double-distilled, charcoal-filtered formula is worth citing again: ***"If a child ever gets the idea into his head that there is something more important to you than he is, then you have no right to be disappointed when something becomes more important to that child than pleasing you."***

ON TRAINING THE CREW

Infants are totally dependent on others for survival. They must be fed, bathed, and clothed by others. Parents--and especially mothers--do these things not because babies are sweet and cuddly (though they are) and not because Moms expect praise or payment (and heaven knows they receive precious little of either) for their acts. They do them because they love their children, and because--because *not* to do them is unthinkable.

But children quickly grow into a stage where they are not only *capable* of tending to some of their own needs, but are fiercely *insistent* on doing so. They want to feed and dress themselves, and draw their own baths. And Mom's woes increase. Nevertheless, this desire, properly encouraged, pays off over the long haul. It did for us.

I came home from the sawmill one rainy Monday afternoon years ago to a classic scene. Toys and books approximately knee-deep from front door to kitchen counter; coats and sweaters 3-deep on 2 chairs and a sofa; a tent/fort/spaceship constructed of card table, blankets, and kitchen chairs blocking entrance to the dining room; noise level on a par with the sawmill's planer and headrig. My wife, who usually met me at the door with a kiss and a, "How was your day, Honey?" was sitting in the rocking chair, silent and motionless except for a disturbing twitch in her left cheek, staring catatonically into the dead ashes of the fireplace.

I was about to ask, "What's for home evening?" This is an activity we tried to hold weekly which involved a short lesson on a scripture, or family living principle, a game, a song or two, and a special refreshment. But I was suddenly overcome with a rash of better judgment. Instead I asked, "Who wants a party for home evening tonight?"

Eight or nine skwibb voices shouted in unison, 'WE DO!!!" (SKWIBB is an endearing acronym we coined which stands for <u>S</u>uper <u>K</u>ids <u>W</u>ith <u>I</u>ncredibly <u>B</u>oisterous <u>B</u>ehavior.) We only had 6 of our own at the time--the extras had probably been recruited by Renee in an effort to generate some extra house-work to fill her idle moments.

"Okay! We'll have a G.I. Party!" Excitement reached fever pitch. I announced that we'd begin immediately. None of them had ever heard of a G.I. party, much less participated in one. "What do we do? One skwibb asked.

"Everyone into the big girls' bedroom." We started there, picking up clothes--dirty ones into the hamper, clean ones into a drawer or closet, toys, books--someone went for the vacuum cleaner--in 10 minutes we were done. "Now what?" On to the next room. Not quite the speed and enthusiasm this time. Then next, and next, right on through the house. About an hour later, we were done. The house looked presentable, if not quite open-house ready. Then, everybody into the living room for discussion and pontificating.

I pointed out that it is not fair for us to expect Mom to do ALL the cleaning, ALL the laundry, ALL the dishes, ALL the cooking and baking, since we ALL helped make the messes, dirty the clothes, and ALL enjoyed the meals, bread, and cookies. It was decreed that thereafter, the first Monday night of every month would be G.I. night. The occupants of any skwibb room clean and orderly enough to pass inspection without any additional attention upon my arrival home would get *double* treats. It was a small price to pay for the chance Renee got to see the floors occasionally.

We stressed that keeping a room in at least semi-acceptable condition was much easier than letting it degenerate into a hygienic disaster area and then trying to reclaim it. This system worked fairly well for several years. It generated an attitude of competitive cooperation (*not* an oxymoron) that taught teamwork, respect and admiration for Mom, and the advantage of staying abreast of chores rather than letting them backlog until the burden becomes overwhelming. (It also got me some emotional, "Thank you, Honeys," over the period this policy was followed.)

PARENTAL SERVICES
ARE SELF-ELIMINATING

Parenting activities often seem like a balancing act. We juggle time around jobs, hobbies, civic and community affairs, and very quickly and (often overwhelmingly) around the interests and activities of our children. Before they go to school, much time is required to clothe, feed, and bathe them. Traditionally, while Dad is off earning the money to buy the shoes, clothes, and groceries the children need, Mom launders, mends, and cooks the same. As children grow in size and interests, music lessons (with recitals and concerts), ball practice (with slates of games), put enormous strain on schedules.

The amount of laundry active teenagers go through in a week is incredible. School clothes, gym clothes, play clothes (for both school-related and other activities), uniforms, work clothes, bath towels, outfits for sock-hops, homecomings, and proms.

And groceries! Besides *regular* meals there are microwaveable dinners (how did mothers of teenagers survive before microwave ovens?), bushels of fruit, barrels of milk, mountains of cookies--all with resulting trash to be disposed of, and dishes to be washed.

Some of the logistical strain is eased when they become licensed drivers, but the cost of gas, tires, insurance, and vehicle upkeep (to say nothing of the resulting worry generated by having teenage drivers) are often a poor trade-off for individual mobility of the kids. When do we have hope that our efforts have been directed toward a worthwhile goal?

He who understands and accepts responsibilities that parenthood places on him begins early to teach his children that *there is a cost for breathing the air on this planet*, and starts by demonstrating that *there are responsibilities connected to membership in the family.* If this is properly done, it is a short step from there to include duties of citizenship in the neighborhood, school, state, and nation. Those who dirty the laundry, dishes, and carpets share the task of cleaning the same. Those who eat food share the task of shopping for it, preparing it, and disposing of garbage associated with those processes.

Children can be taught early to share cleaning chores; to fold and stow their own clothes; to fix simple snacks and meals; and to be considerate of the space and schedules of others. Unfortunate indeed is the college-age student or military basic trainee who has *not* learned to rinse toothpaste and shaving cream from the sink as a courtesy to the next user--because he *will* learn it from his roommates--harshly, and at volume, and perhaps at the cost of a life-long friendship. Parents who have done their job well send into the world young *adults*, (not perpetual children) who *can* and *will* do their own shopping, laundry, and housekeeping *because they have been taught to pull their weight.* There is an adage to the effect that giving a man a fish feeds him for a day, but teaching him how to fish feeds him for a lifetime. By the same token, the parent who has taught his or her own children domestic survival skills produces adults who can shift for themselves.

Grown children who have *not* learned the requisite lessons are left with two options:
(1) Either they shift their dependence to a mate or to an agency willing to assume the role of doting parent or
(2) They live in the inevitable squalor that is generated by indolence and total dependence.

ON CREATIVITY & CONSTRAINTS

One of our children was a precocious artist, showing ability to draw animals in remarkable perspective at an age when his friends were still drawing stick figures. A friend of ours, who happened to be a certified art teacher, was visiting one day and marveled at the child's ability.

"I'm glad to see you provide drawing paper and pencils, rather than those store-bought coloring books. It is a more creative method of expression."

"Oh, we provide those too. Sometimes he uses them. It depends on his mood."

"But this way encourages individuality and imagination," the friend commented. "It takes little creativity to color a picture someone else has drawn."

I replied, "Of course, art created under these conditions can be beautiful and aesthetically pleasing. But it is important to learn that for some artistic creations to be attractive, the methods used to create them must be tightly structured. The colors for Cinderella's gown and coach are up to the child, but for the finished picture to be appealing, those colors must stay inside lines that *someone else* drew. Young artists need to learn that principle, too."

I thought about this conversation often, as younger siblings came along, and struggled with the skills of hand/eye coordination--and the social skills required for producing acceptable (and even artistic) social behavior. Children often generate dialogue while playing house, cowboys, or other childhood pastimes that show imagination and creative skill. They even invent their own games, improvising and revising rules at whim, and continue them for hours.

But for some games, rules must be established, understood, and followed by all the players. The quality of the game depends on player performance while *operating within the confines of the rules.*

In organized games, referees render decisions regarding rule interpretation and the play itself. Generally there is no appeal on an umpire's call. Failure of a player to accept the ruling of an official may cost a player the right to continue playing--and in extreme cases can cost the protestor's team the game by forfeiture.

Children must learn the nature of rules--which ones are arbitrary and flexible; which are rigid and universal. They need to learn this early and convincingly, because as surely as they achieve adulthood, they *will* learn it. If they have been allowed to view traffic laws (just to cite an example) as being matters of mutual consent of their circle of friends, they face some harsh disappointment at the calls of society's legal umpires.

Parents--and the children they allow to "draw" their own pictures for senior skip day or prom night activities--often learn to their mutual dismay that the coloring books society has drawn up to cover these situations are graded harshly when the acts of those behavioral artists "go outside the lines."

UNTHUMPING NOSES

Our youngest daughter crawled up into my lap one day to begin the familiar buttering-up process that inevitably leads to the asking of a favor, or some particularly desired permission to be granted. Side-tracked momentarily by my teasing, she thumped the end of my nose (a frequently used form of mock aggression), then remembered her original purpose. She quickly placed the tip of her thumping finger on the spot, and in an exaggerated reversed motion, "un-thumped" my nose.

Then followed (with requisite mock severity) an explanation that a nose-- especially a Dad-nose, once thumped, could never be un-thumped. I had frequently explained to this daughter (as she emphatically wiped off a slobbery kiss) that a Dad-kiss cannot be erased; that like a tattoo, it remains forever, and all efforts to remove it are wasted. In the moments following this exchange, it occurred to me that among the important realities parents must teach their children is the awareness *of*, and appreciation *for* which noses can and cannot be "un-thumped."

Children quickly understand that neither balloons nor bubbles, once popped, can ever be un-popped. They understand only a little later that these irreversible events are not tragedies, since there are other balloons, and there is more bubble mix in the bottle.

As a child grows, experiences life--get his bubbles popped, and his nose thumped, he needs to have it pointed out to him (by someone who loves him, and who has a sincere interest in his immediate and future happiness) that *his* acts, decisions, and choices must all be weighed in the scale of "un-do-ability."

The scale of discipline that parents use should reflect this concept. A toy left out can be put away later (and if it is not, the worst consequence of such irresponsibility is a mild irritation to Mom). But what if the toy in question is a roller skate that was left on a flight of stairs? Consequences of the magnitude of this sort of omission may not be "un-do-able," and should be factored in to whatever discipline is invoked. A stolen item can be returned or paid for; a chore left unperformed can be done later with minimal damage done; many tasks poorly executed can be redone with greater attention to detail.

But the hurting of a friend's person or feelings is harder to undo. A slanderous lie, once spread, is not retrievable. A person killed or maimed by a speeding drunk, or an under-skilled driver remains dead or paralyzed, grief and apologies notwithstanding.

It is not just an ironic word play to suggest that the repentance process involves our own "un-doing"--the undoing of ignoble, thoughtless, or even deliberate misdeeds. Because some deeds simply *cannot be* undone--some noses cannot be un-thumped--you need to teach your children to be very selective about which ones they *do* thump--and how hard--and why.

MILESTONES TO MANHOOD

When does a boy become a man? Where is the boy who has not looked up at men--fathers, grandfathers, neighbors, athletic heroes--and envied their independence, strength, control, size, and facial hair--and wondered how long it would be until *he* enjoyed all the advantages of manhood?

My first encounter with the vicissitudes of adulthood came when the cashier at the walk-in theater began charging me 65 cents to see movies that I could have seen the previous summer for a quarter. I realized that with my limited allowance, being this step closer to adulthood was hardly an advantage.

Come back with me, those of you who see yourselves as adults (reaching woman-hood is doubtless as trying and traumatic for our sisters as achieving manhood is for us), and let's re-examine some of the *milestones* that marked our passage.

When one has reached the age of 16, the State of Oregon accepts that his or her judgment has advanced to the point where he or she can be entrusted with solo operation of an automobile. Without belaboring numbers and insurance rates, anyone would agree that having celebrated 16 birthdays does not *ipso facto* qualify anyone to drive anything--(with the possible exception of parents crazy!).

The liquor commissions of most states use 21 years as age of sufficient judgment to be considered adults. Many high school students are using alcohol prior to reaching 18, and some are well along the road to alcoholism by the time they reach 21. Would that there were some way to determine accurately *who* possesses sufficient judgment, and *when*, to receive liquor control cards!

Our lawmakers have determined that 18 year-olds have sufficient judgment to be allowed to vote. Looking at performance records of some of our voters--and the officials they elect--makes one wonder whether 50 might not be a safer voting age. Clearly, some *never* acquire the judgment, insight, value system, and soberness to vote intelligently. Still, there must be some criterion, and age seems fairer than most.

High school graduation? Graduates in a given high school class may range from 12 to 50 years of age, with measurable common sense and sense of responsibility distrib-uted randomly.

Marriage? Arguably, those who have successfully weathered several years of married life have gained some insights conducive to making wiser decisions. But every year marriages fail that have lasted several decades, and some that began with teen-age brides mark golden and even diamond anniversaries.

The Apostle Paul said, "When I was a child, I spake as a child, I thought as a child, I understood as a child. But when I became a man, I *put away childish things*." (1st Cor. 13:11)

We become men (or women) in proportion to the childish things we put away. Learning to settle differences in the sandbox or on the playground, is a more meaningful milestone than completing kindergarten (or even high school), and many whom we acknowledge as adults have never acquired this skill.

How many voters have used their franchise to elect those who promise to enact legislation to subsidize abortions? They thus attempt to relieve the unchaste of the responsibilities inherent with expressing one's sexuality. *It can't be done*. It has been wisely noted that while we *can* dodge our responsibilities, there is *no way* to dodge the *consequences* of dodging responsibilities.

The milestones we pass need to be recognized for what they *are*, and for what they are *not*. They are certainly not bestowals of omniscience or omnipotence. Abuse of driving privileges, drinking privileges, and voting privileges bring grief beyond measure to irresponsible people, as well as to those around them.

Auto-crash quadriplegics, alcoholics, unwed mothers, AIDS patients--these, for the most part, represent those for whom *milestones* have become *millstones* because of their failure to "put away childish things."

Let us train and instruct our children so that their milestones will become *stepping* stones to adulthood, parenthood, and happiness, rather than *mill*stones around their necks.

FEARS & CHILDREN

One thing children struggle with--perhaps *most* of what children struggle with--is *fear*. Even peer pressure is essentially fear of not being accepted by one's friends. Some children fear (for good reason!) being abandoned by one or both parents; some fear having a weakness or imperfection discovered by their peers. Some fears are justified. Ironically, many things parents fear in behalf of their children, children fear not at all. The thought of no-hands bicycling, skateboard injuries, playing with matches, and the climbing of high rocks and trees worry children but little, but cause panic in parents.

Good parents help children learn to cope with fear, and to get a handle on what things they are justified in fearing. An initial step in dealing effectively with fear is to properly define it.

Webster defines fear as, "a distressing emotion aroused by impending danger, evil, or pain, whether real or imagined." Fear is often equated with cowardice, but these terms are only related, not synonymous. Peter Ustinov observed, "Courage is often fueled by lack of insight, whereas cowardice in many cases is based on good information." Fear may perhaps best be described in terms of its opposites.

Courage is generally accepted as the opposite of fear. Plato defined courage as, "wisdom concerning danger." This definition implies that the object of our fear may well constitute a genuine threat--one worthy of being avoided. If courage is "wisdom concerning danger," it is fair to define fear as, "proper respect, or wise regard for danger." This perspective gives us a place to start in showing our children the correlation between fear and genuine peril.

Children have legitimate reason to fear many of the things they encounter. Con-versely, many are of the "boogey-man" sort, and overcoming fear of such phobias is one of the marks of maturity. Reflect on which category you would have placed the following as a 6-year old, as a 10-year old, or as a late teen-ager, then consider into which you would place them today: The dark, deep water, and no-hands bicycling. Strangers, policemen, and excessive speed. Doctors, dentists, and strange dogs. Add to the list peer pressure, being alone, being laughed at, and rejection by the college of your choice.

All of these things contain elements for which you may have had legitimate reason to be concerned. But some have the potential of not only being unworthy of your terror, but of contributing elements essential to happy, fulfilling lives.

There are effective methods for overcoming and dealing with specific fears. Fear of bullies can be overcome with acquisition of self-defense techniques. One's fear of water can be allayed with swimming lessons. But wherever there exists an unreasonable fear in a child, or if no "respect for danger" exists where it really ought, there are tools parents can use to engender that respect.

First and second of these tools are faith and knowledge. Every child has faith in his parents (until the parents convince the child that it is undeserved); it is built in by nature. By proper use of this you can provide the information, the technical data, and the knowledge to put any feared concept into proper perspective.

It doesn't happen immediately, but that's okay. You have some 18 to 20 years to do it. But if *you* don't do it, it won't get done.

MERCENARY PARENTING

The rearing of children is an enterprise one may approach from many different directions. Unfortunately, many have "bought in" to parenting with no previously determined goal, nor methods to achieve it, even if they have one in mind. For such as these, tactics and methodology tend to be arbitrary, with the only discernable reference point being maintaining of parental sanity until "those brats are big enough to evict."

Too many children come into the world as unplanned, unwanted--even as resented intrusions into the lives of parents committed to the pursuit of hedonistic existence. And, as with other consumer markets, a willing, avaricious, and mercenary bunch of suppliers has materialized and expanded to fill the demand for care these children desperately need. The late 20th century gave birth to a variety of agencies designed to profit from this order of parent and the children they generate. Such agencies provide needed services to these children--protection and supervision--but they undercut their own value by salving the consciences of those who would abrogate parental obligations and responsibilities.

They call themselves by such titles as Day Care Centers, Nurseries, Pre-schools, Head-Start Programs, and other euphemistic titles that connote being more advantageous to the children attending them than is the care and training received at the hands of their own parents.

Kahlil Gibran said, "He brings disaster upon his nation who never sows a seed, or lays a brick, or weaves a garment, but makes politics his occupation." Paraphrasing Gibran, and applying his rationale to the area of rearing children, I say, "Woe unto the children of a nation that hires laboratory and classroom trained 'behavioral scientists' to dictate the raising of its children."

This is not to say that those politicians--or those child behavior specialists--know *nothing* of value, or even that they are by definition evil. It is simply that *nobody* can provide "parenting" to a child as effectively as his parents.

Anyone else *can* provide food, housing, protection, and instruction, all of which are *elements* of parenting. But the *best* parenting *package* is available from one source only. Anyone who believes otherwise is not paying attention to what has been happening to children in this country lately.

Numbers for teenage gangs (and related crimes), teen pregnancies, STDs, abortions, drug addiction, alcoholism, and suicide are more alarming now than they have ever been. These mercenary agencies aren't getting the job done! Not that this is their fault--they are simply not equipped *to* do it--*they are not the parents of our children.* It is as though we are hiring brick masons to do our gardening.

Mothers bear children; no one but mothers can. *Fathers* sire them; no one else can. *These* are parents, and only these can "parent." Yes, others *can* feed them, change their diapers, and bathe them. But only parents *can* provide the whole parenting package. *Parents* aren't getting the job done! *Much of the reason is that too many of them mistakenly think that they can hire it done while they are on a golf course, or are competing in a bowling league, or are chairing the League of Women Voters, or working to pay for a new motor home.*

FLIGHT & MATURATION

Man has envied birds and other airborne life forms from the beginning of time. A look at the birth and development of heavier-than-air flight, the mastery of aerodynamic principles, and innovations in engine mechanics reveals some intriguing analogies to the human maturation process.

The kite represents man's first successful effort to overcome gravitational forces. For a kite to fly effectively, three elements must factor in, coupled to the expertise of the pilot. First is the wind. Ideally, gentle to moderate breezes make kite flying exciting and intriguing, and provide the motive force and sufficient unpredictability to keep it interesting. Second is the design of the kite. The faces of the kite must resist the wind and balance the kite as air currents eddy around it. Third is tension on the string. Too little tension and gravity overcomes the lift of the wind; too much tension and the fabric shreds and loses its aerodynamic integrity. Cut or release the string and even the most cleverly designed and artistically pleasing kite comes out of the air with all the grace and glory of a crippled duck.

The limitation of kites is that even though they can be designed to lift a man, they can't take him anywhere except UP. So manned flight remained a dream for centuries, though the principles of aerodynamics were understood long before man's mechanical skills had produced engines capable of providing motive power to his kites. Designs of viable aircraft were found in the notes of Leonardo DaVinci--only the motor was lacking.

As the Wright brothers and others experimented with primitive flying machines, they were essentially adding power to box kites. As engine design improved, so did air frame technology. Within 45 years of the first powered flight men were flying at supersonic speeds. In 20 more they landed on the moon.

Toddlers, children, adolescents--all long to "fly." Prudent parents understand the dangers of exposing them to excessive winds, and the importance of proper tension on the line. They ensure that their charges understand the basics of both tethered and free flight. Ideally, by the time the string is cut, adequate power has been installed. Navigational instruments are in place; their use and importance grasped by young pilots.

Good parents would not have their child remain a "kite" forever--but neither will they release the string before adequate flight training has been given, and sufficient preparation for free flight has been made.

The laws of aerodynamics and gravity are unforgiving laws, as are the laws of human interaction. Knowledge of these laws and principles alone ensures no one's safe flight. The laws must be *understood* and *obeyed*--indeed, they cannot be broken. We can only break ourselves against them. The instruments must be read, and their readings applied. The authority of the Air Traffic Controller must be recognized, and held inviolate.

Let any of these concepts be ignored and disaster will surely follow.

BUOYS & BEACONS

The practice of marking navigational hazards has helped countless pilots throughout history. Channel markers and buoys warn of reefs and rocks and as reference points by which to plot one's course. Lighthouses, visible for many miles, serve as beckoning beacons to ships far at sea, then as the harbor is neared, the course can be altered to avoid grounding ships on the rocks on which the lighthouses stand.

Nautical and aviation markers are illuminated with specifically colored lights. To the trained navigator, the lights communicate important information beyond the location and direction of the marker to the observer. *Mistaking one marker for another can be as disastrous for a sailor or an aviator as finding no marker at all.*

Much of the task of parenting involves instructing our children on identification and selection of buoys and guideposts, and differentiating between buoys and beacons. Many and varied are "stars" that shine in the eyes of our teenagers. Some are athletes, some recording artists, some actors. They are highly visible; their signals listened to; their positions sought after; their life styles, language, and modes of dress copied.

Reading the weekly personality-oriented magazines and super-market tabloids should be warning enough for anyone to be cautious about using these shining lights as homing beacons rather than shoal markers. Here is a major league outfielder, paid millions for his ability to hit home runs--benched, fined, undergoing drug rehab; or a hoopster who learns to his dismay that the magic he performs on the basketball court can not conjure away the fatal rip in the hull of his sleek, fast-lane craft. Here is a talented young actor, dead of a drug overdose. The list could run to pages.

I remember Hy Gardner's interview with Elvis Presley. Elvis was at the peak of his career. Gardner asked Elvis for his opinions on various topics. Presley's response was refreshing. He said in effect, "I'm an entertainer, not a social scientist. My opinion on these things is worth no more than anyone else's." The sad saga of his subsequent preoccupation with drugs, and his death related the abuse of them, is testimony enough that *his* counsel on how the rest of us should conduct our lives would have been suspect.

Most of the reefs in the sea of life have been marked, some by the Harbormaster, and some by the wrecked hulks of those who would not heed. The buoys are lit, and for the most part, easily recognized. Teenagers deserve to be taught to select wisely which ones to "home in" on and which to use as reference points as they navigate their way around reefs and shoals. To paraphrase Stringfellow Barr, "He who won't take his instruction from the buoys is doomed to take it from the rocks."

FORCE: ITS USE AND THREAT

I took an education methods class at the University of Utah from a man who had been an educator for 30-odd years. His job now was to give aspiring teachers an idea of the challenges they were facing, and the tools with which to meet them.

He told of an experience he'd had early in his career as a junior high school principal. The school drew its student body from several grade schools, including the one where he had spent years as a teacher. From this school came Charlie.

Charlie had terrorized every teacher he'd ever had. He had, in fact, driven two of them to early retirement, including one who was a noted disciplinarian. The principal's tasks included evaluating his novice teachers, including Mr. Jones, a first-year geography teacher, whose misfortune it was to have Charlie in his class. He told us, "I was anxious to see how he would fare with Charlie, because of his newness and Charlie's reputation. I knew it would be a momentous experience--world-class brat versus novice teacher--the classic confrontation. Whatever the outcome, I knew it would be interesting."

"I entered the classroom and sat in the rear, trying to be as inconspicuous as possible. Mr. Jones began his presentation. Three minutes into it Charlie began cutting up. Mr. Jones laid his chalk in the chalk tray and walked back to Charlie's seat without interrupting the flow of his presentation. He placed a hand on Charlie's shoulder and whispered a few words in his ear, then returned to the front of the room. He then proceeded to conduct a lively discussion--with eighth graders--on the universally loathed subject of world geography--in an upstairs room of a 40-year old school house lacking air conditioning, on a hot, September afternoon--a presentation complete with provocative questions, insightful answers, laughter, and understanding nods for the next 45 minutes--during which Charlie never made another disruptive gesture nor inappropriate comment.

"Amazing! I gave him 'excellent' on all areas of the evaluation," he told us. "I'd never witnessed a more polished performance. This guy was 3 months out of college and 2 weeks into his career, and was already a master teacher. But most impressive was the way he handled Charlie, and I told him so. 'What did you say to him?' I asked."

"Well, I'm not so sure it's as much *what* I said, as the *way* I said it," Mr. Jones replied.

"Whatever! I want to know what you said, and how you said it--I'm going to patent it and get rich. There are teachers who would kill for that kind of control, so I know they'll buy it!"

Mr. Jones shared his secret. "I don't know whether you could see from your angle that I had my hand on his shoulder as I whispered to him--but I'm sure you couldn't see my thumb under his collar bone to the second knuckle. What I said was, 'You listen to me, you little b----d, if you make one more peep while my boss is back there doing this evaluation, I'm going to throw you headfirst from this second story window. Do you understand me?' I guess the little b----d understood."

We all chuckled, then the principal-turned-professor put into perspective the lesson he wanted us to learn. "Now, I'm not suggesting that you throw kids out of windows. What I want you to remember is that it was not necessary for Mr. Jones to do that to establish control. All he had to do was to make Charlie *believe* that he was not only willing, he was anxious to do it, and friends, (he here adopted the raised hands, eyes-upwards posture of mock prayer) Charlie *BELIEVED!!*"

The punishments we administered to our children were applied with this *concept* in mind. I never threw any of them out the window, of course, or even threatened to. But I made sure they understood that, "If you do that again, I'll do *this* again--do you believe me?" And they believed. And because they believed, I didn't have to punish any of them for the last several years they were home.

WHY & BECAUSE

Justifying oneself to a child can be an exercise in futility. No matter how rational and necessary a decision may appear to you, your child often seems to be a bottomless well of, "But Daddy, WHY...?"

I remember as a child nagging and tormenting Mom until she would finally relent. Sometimes I felt a genuine sense of victory, sure that my budding arguing skills had carried the day; that justice and fair play had prevailed. Little did I appreciate what had *really* happened on those occasions. My whining and sniveling had simply eroded Mom's defenses to the point where she would consent just for the chance to hold on to the last remaining shreds of her sanity!

Dad was an entirely different sort of challenge. No adolescent on the planet was ever going to out-argue Dad. This was partly because of the enormous scope of his knowledge, but mostly because he never felt compelled to justify decrees to knot-headed kids. Not that he *couldn't*, you understand--he just *didn't*. And it is hard for a kid to make any headway arguing with a sphinx. His sole justification for countless vetoes of my adolescent enterprises was, "Because I said so."

Many times as a youth, I vowed that if I ever had kids of my own, I'd never be guilty of copping out with a, "Because I said so," refusal. I've broken that vow. No, that is not accurate. I've bent it, tried to hammer it straight, then finally decided to deal with it realistically. I got a cutting torch, chopped into tiny fragments, and scrapped it.

But I'm justified.

My vow was made originally from the perspective and experience-log of a *kid*, whose main goal in life was to be amused and entertained. Any program, obstacle, or seemingly arbitrary decree from Dad that got in the way of that, seemed unfair.

Kids (actually, people of whatever age) evaluate new information by comparing it with past experience. The limited experience of a kid has no way of letting him relate to the fears parents have of their son's acquiring a motorcycle, or playing organized football with his 106-pound body, or of their daughter's going to a drive-in movie with a sailor home from a year at sea.

Arguing in instances like these, *or* issuing adamant decrees will create friction and feelings. I have no solution to the discomfort it causes, but there is a rationale that I have found helpful in salving the raw nerves resulting from the differing desires of myself and my children.

I really do take parenting seriously. I tried for over 30 years to demonstrate to my children that I had their well-being--their long- and short-term interests at heart. This kept parent/adolescent confrontations to a minimum. Still, there were times...

The marketable reason for a parent's veto is often of the sort, "You can't go (or *do*, or *have*...) because your chores aren't done, or because you were late last time, or because your grades are slipping." In most instances these are only *incidentally* related to the *ultimate* justification caring parents can invoke. The purpose in denying permission is not sadistic glee in thwarting the child's chance to have fun. It is to teach him the responsibility of getting his chores done, or the importance of punctuality, or the importance of worthy effort. Often, it is simply to *protect* him from dangers he lacks the maturity and experience to understand.

If, "Because I said so," really means, "I said so *because*..." (And here fill in the *real*, long-term reason), it is not the cop-out I thought it was 60+ years ago. And whether it is adequately explained at the time of the decree or not, most children will eventually recognize the fairness and wisdom of it.

CHOICES FOR CHUCK

During the time I spent in the timber products labor force, I met some fascinating people. Chuck was one of the most interesting. During random conversations I learned that he had grown up in New York City's infamous lower east side. As a high school drop-out, he had ridden freight trains across the country both ways by the time he was 16. His education in the formal sense was limited, but he was articulate and literate in his conversation. He told interesting stories about his adventures, and he told them well.

While feeding a veneer dryer together one night, we began discussing things we had read. He quoted a passage from *The Rubaiyat*, and when I confessed that I had not read it he was outraged. "You claim to be a literature major, and haven't even read *The Rubaiyat?*"

I could offer little in my defense except to ask where in the world a high school sophomore drop-out would ever encounter the writings of someone like Omar Khayyam. He sort of smiled, gazed at some distant image invisible to me, and replied, "Well, Larry, there comes a time when counting the rivets in the ceiling of your cell ceases to provide entertainment, and you'll do anything--even read *The Rubaiyat*--for a change."

He never confided the details of the events that led to his incarceration and his stretch in solitary. He did mention a prison librarian who "allowed" him to cut his literary teeth on 2 volumes: *Crime and Punishment,* by Dostoyevsky, and a collegiate dictionary. It took him 3 months to read the book, but towards the end he found he was looking up fewer and fewer words.

When he completed it and returned it for exchange, she said, "No, you read it again." So he did. Next was *War and Peace,* Then followed an eclectic variety (selected by the librarian) which Chuck admitted opened a world to him that he never knew existed. At some point *The Rubaiyat* came under his scrutiny.

Later we got into another discussion regarding the relative merits of socialized medicine. When I voiced my skepticism of its practicality, he was again outraged. He defended his position of advocacy by citing the experience of having known kids who died of infected rat bites because they lacked $5 for penicillin and band-aids.

Over the span of many nights we discussed the evils of poverty, organized crime, bigotry, illiteracy--and the validity of arguments. He had experienced the *reality* of societal injustices. My opinions were based on objective, as opposed to subjective experience, and on exposure to theories and abstract principles.

We debated at length the issue of environmental impact on the finished human product. He quoted *statistics*; I argued *concepts*. He cited studies; I pointed to exceptions. My position has not changed. If anything, I feel more strongly than ever that while such factors as environment and heredity *contribute* to our individual make-ups, the essence of any human life is *the sum of the decisions he or she has made.*

If we are destined to be *products of our environment*, how do we explain that from such "deprived" environments as Hell's Kitchen, rural Appalachia, and the mid-West dust-bowl of the 1930's, there have arisen giants of humanity? On the other hand, how to explain that from the privileged, moneyed environments of the rich and famous there come some of those who, though born heirs of the silver spoon, wind up as refuse on the scrap heaps of society? If environment and heredity are *the* vital factors, why the vast difference in levels of productivity, accomplishment, and value systems of siblings reared in the same households, and neighbors who attend the same schools, enjoy the same diversions, and whose parents work the same jobs?

Chuck's childhood environment exposed him to a value system that rewarded the ruthless and victimized the vulnerable. He had ample opportunity to exploit cleverness, strength, and ruthlessness at the expense of the weak, the compassionate, and the slow to learn. When his crimes caught up with him and he went to prison, he was placed in an environment that many regard as a finishing school for those who are of that mind set.

Being force-fed uplifting and enlightening literature was no guarantee that his behavior would change. But somewhere along the crooked road he was walking *he made a <u>decision</u>*. While it may be argued that working plywood is hardly an elite profession, it certainly is nobler than mugging bag ladies and robbing fruit vendors.

A convicted burglar I met during my stint as a correctional officer described the circumstances of his arrest. He had burglarized a warehouse and stolen a station wagon full of goods. He had made his getaway undetected, but was flagged down by a highway patrolmen who had noticed that his seat belt was not fastened. His tools were behind the seat; his wagon was full of stereo components; he had a prior record; there he was, back in the slammer. When asked whether he had learned a lesson, his reply was predictable. "Hell, yes! I'll never go anywhere again as long as I live without fastening my seat belt."

Given the same experiences, we, for whatever reason, learn different lessons. One learns, "I was wrong to rob that warehouse." Another learns, "If only I'd been a little more clever I'd have been home free--so next time, I'll *be* more clever."

Both physical environment and genetics obviously contribute to our make-up, but there is something *unique* and *individual* that manifests itself in the way we *respond* to stimuli, and in how we *decide* to deal with life. However influential these factors are, we are, above all else, *products of the decisions we've made.*

SCHOOLS & EDUCATION

Public schools came into being in this country because enough influential people believed it was the responsibility of the *masses* to ensure that the youth of America could learn to read, write, and count. Up until the late nineteenth century, public schools were effective enough at teaching these skills that often boys and girls who had completed 8 years of grammar school could apply for teaching credentials and begin to teach students themselves.

A combination of forces has complicated the role of public schools. The information boom of the post-World War I era has necessitated expanding curricula to include more detailed and up-to-date classes in sciences, industrial arts, and business related skills. The strength of the NEA lobbyists put the education profession into a position of unprecedented influence. The impact of modern psychology was manifested as the concepts of behavior modification, and positive/negative reinforcement, etc., were adopted by educators and applied to classroom settings.

As the post World War II shift towards two-income families gained momentum, parents began to see schools as day-care facilities, baby-sitters, and surrogate parents.

We compare curricula of today's high schools with those of 75 to 100 years ago and see some predictable and necessary changes. But when we compare the *readiness* of today's high school graduates to function in their world with that of their grandparents' ability to function in theirs, the contrast is appalling.

Many studies show that 20% of today's high school graduates are functionally illiterate. We're not talking about being uninformed on the latest developments in gene-splicing or space exploration--*1 in 5 can't read a newspaper*! And for this we vilify the schools, we crucify curriculum planners, and ask, "Why can't Johnny's teacher teach?"

Consider: Where once we expected our teachers to teach our kids to read, write, and cipher, and hopefully to instill in them a sense of citizenship and responsibility, we now expect them to teach our elementary students about everything from oral hygiene to ozone layers, our junior high students everything from badminton to birth control, and high school students everything from driving cars to demonology. And all this while dragging them all over the state for ball games, festival promotions, chess tournaments, essay contests, and who knows what else? It's amazing, given the scope of this madness, that the education system does as well as it does.

And if it's not enough to expect them to teach this incredible spectrum of modern -ologies--we insist that they do it in a bedlam generated by recalcitrant youngsters whose parents have been so busy working to make payments on the water-ski boat or motor home that they haven't taken time to teach their children the first principles of common courtesy--and these same parents go apoplectic if a teacher attempts to discipline their child! If teachers could spend their energies focusing on their respective fields instead of having to referee playground squabbles and monitor restrooms for drug and alcohol abusers, their jobs would be more rewarding and the results more dramatic. They can't teach kids to master academic material if the students haven't been taught by their parents when it's time to sit down and pay attention.

WHAT WE WANT & WHY WE WANT IT

Once a man presenting a business opportunity to me asked what I would do if I had a million dollars. I told him I would buy an adequately-sized house well enough furnished that my wife would not need to feel embarrassed to invite guests into; a roadworthy Skwibbmobile, some books, and probably some travel tickets.

"Then what?" he persisted.

"That's it," I assured him.

"How about a college fund for your kids?" he asked.

"If I had $10,000,000, I'd not put a dime of it into a college fund for my child-ren," I told him.

The man was an educational professional. He was shocked. "I thought you were a pro-education man," he said. Well, I am. But I don't equate education with 4-year social bacchanals paid for by dad. What I desire for my children in terms of education, and their attitude towards it, is difficult for me to articulate.

In the movie, "Dead Poet's Society," Neil Perry's father wants him to be a doctor. He has planned, sacrificed, saved; then threatened, intimidated, and cajoled Neil all his life to ensure that it would happen. He never considers what Neil might want, much less what might be best for him. Mr. Perry wants Neil to be a doctor. End of discussion.

I wanted for my children to realize that *any* endeavor *they* choose to pursue will please me if it pleases their Creator first, themselves second, and then whomever else their choice happens to benefit.

I have never wanted for my kids just to have, "gone to college." I wanted them to understand that the acquisition of worthwhile learning isn't restricted to college campuses, and that if time in some professor's class is worthwhile, the effort it takes to pay for it ought to be worth as much to the child/student as it is to me.

Not to devalue the learning dispensed by colleges, but I have lived long enough to know that *not all that is worthwhile and true is taught there, and of more concern, not all that is taught there is worthwhile or true.*

I wanted my children to be able to discern the difference between nuggets of knowledge and fool's gold, and to appreciate that truth is as valuable coming from a tenderfoot Boy Scout as it is from an instructor with a Ph.D.

I wanted most for them to know that their ultimate worth as human beings (and certainly the value of their education) will not be determined by how I choose to spend what money I have.

Some of the things I learned in college have been useful and applicable in the disciplining and instruction of my own children. I would likely have gained much more from my classroom instruction had my *motives* for attending those classes been so focused. Whatever my children genuinely want in terms of either education or careers, I hope their motives will be nobler than mine were, and that they will measure their success in these areas by a loftier standard than either the dollars they earn, or pats on the back by a doting father.

DECISIONS & SUFFERING

The most intense of all human suffering comes as the result of someone's poor decisions. Tsunamis in Indonesia, Earthquakes in California, floods in the Midwest, blizzards on the east coast, volcanoes in Washington, hurricanes along the Gulf Coast--all get our attention. These events cause Presidents and governors to activate relief agencies, declare disaster areas, and issue pleas for compassionate co-operation from citizens.

Obviously, people don't cause these cataclysmic events, so arguably these happenings might be viewed as exceptions to my generalization. But in terms of both intensity and numbers, it still holds up.

For those who have lost homes, businesses, property, or loved ones--there is inconvenience, discomfort, and suffering. But compared to trauma inflicted upon the population as a result of criminal activity, drug and alcohol abuse, and broken homes, these so-called natural disasters are minor setbacks. Homes and businesses can be rebuilt. Property can be replaced. Wounds caused by the loss of these things eventually heal. Floodwaters recede, snow melts, and spring returns.

One need only talk to the parents of an abducted child, or the survivor of a drive-by shooting to put the trauma of violent crime ahead of house fires or a collapsed freeway cloverleaf. Or talk to medics and patients in alcohol and drug rehab facilities to determine that many of the heaviest human burdens are self-inflicted. See a terminal AIDS patient, or a derelict adolescent seeking acceptance and self-esteem in aberrant behavior, and you realize that *poor choices* cause more severe and more numerous cases of suffering than earthquakes, floods, and forest fires combined.

High school seniors are counseled extensively regarding college and career selection. Military recruiters are invited in to discuss what service to one's country can return in terms of career training and educational funds. Great emphasis is placed on making wise choices. Claims are often made that future happiness and sense of accomplishment are dependent on these decisions. High school curricula all over the nation are currently undergoing radical changes designed to necessitate serious reflection and goal selection by students in their early teens. They will need to be thinking maturely about educational and career choices before they begin to drive!

Let's cut to the bottom line, and ask a pertinent question. Given all the choices facing adolescents, is it possible to identify *which* decision will *most radically* affect their chances for lasting happiness? Can it be hoped that there is a single answer, applicable to all, regardless of occupational aspirations or consumer preferences?

A look at any newspaper should be enough to satisfy even the most worldly that acquisition of money doesn't guarantee happiness, nor does money of itself provide a sense of accomplishment. High-income entertainers and athletes slip into drug and alcohol abuse in numbers way out of proportion to the rest of society. Suicide numbers for this group are equally disturbing. So why all the focus on choosing a lucrative career? Neither money, nor the sense of fulfillment from the profession that generates it, assures happiness.

Talk to the obviously happy, to the obviously unhappy, and here's what you will find: *The single decision that will most likely affect your chances for lasting happiness will be your choice of mates.* Choose poorly, and you set yourself up for heartache that cannot be numbed--not with dollars, not with toys, and not with divorce settlements. Choose poorly, and prepare yourself for ongoing conflict that will cover every phase of your life from dinner menu to the disciplining of your children. Choose poorly, and join the ranks of those who come to refer to their partners as, "my ball and chain."

Choose wisely, and enjoy the support of one who understands, values, and complements your differences, and yet cherishes the oneness he or she shares with you.

By "choice of mates," I do not restrict it to the one you choose to marry, though volumes could be spent on this facet of adult agency. I'm talking about your choice of bed partners--even the choice *to* share your bed. *Choose poorly, and no matter what other circumstances you enjoy or endure, your capacity for future happiness will be thereby forever limited.* * The possible consequences of sexual activity are so profound and irreversible that in this, of all human decisions, wise, methodical, and conscientious choices *must* be made. Fathering or bearing a child is the ultimate in human creative acts, and allowing or inviting anyone to join us in this venture should inspire our noblest selective effort, both of partners and of circumstances.

On the other hand, the risk of sexually transmitted diseases ought to inspire a sense of caution bordering on paranoia, because the results can be devastating. You can't abort AIDS. You can't abort babies without risking physical and psychological consequences--none of which will bring you happiness, lasting or any other kind. Results of our sexual decisions will be forever enjoyed, or forever *endured.*

Almost any other decision we make may be altered or revoked. We change careers, relocate, reinvest savings with a sense of adventure and excitement. No feeling person changes mates (whether or not children are involved) without a profound sense of loss and failure--without experiencing emotional and psychological agony.

A friend of mine served in Viet Nam with Special Forces. When his first marriage broke up, he confided that though the action he'd seen as a Green Beret had exposed him to emotional and physical trauma impossible to describe, it wasn't the first lesson in suffering compared to the dissolution of his marriage. "And if it was that hard for me," he concluded, "I can't even imagine what is was for my kids."

Illustrations of why we need to make wise choices in all our adult decisions surround us. Poor choices cause suffering to ourselves, to our children, and to society. We need to gather all the information we can get, and analyze it carefully, before we commit ourselves in something that will be *the* major factor in our future happiness.

Yet there are men and boys who spend more time analyzing data from *Motor Trend* Magazine before buying their first car than they spend considering when and with whom to surrender their virginity. And there are women and girls who worry more about the size of the engagement ring they are offered than they are with the quality of the one who offers it.

*(See again the Appendix on page 185)

THE PROBLEM IS THE FOCUS

My junior high math teacher taught us more than math. She gave us priceless lessons in problem analysis and solution, and in semantics. She told us that many of the problems we encounter are complicated by *failure to identify and define the real problem*. Further, that we often impose limitations on possible solutions that are not inherent in the "givens" stated in the exercise. She presented us with an example.

"I have in my hand two standard issue coins, minted in the U.S., total value of which is 35 cents, and one of them is not a dime. What are the coins?"

We struggled with it for several minutes. We asked her to repeat the "givens." We challenged the possibility of a solution. She assured us that there was one. Finally someone arrived at the answer. The coins were a quarter and a dime.

We protested. "But you said one wasn't a dime."

She conceded. "*One* of them isn't," she replied, "it's a quarter. The problem here is that you all *heard*, '*Neither* is a dime,' a condition not stated in the 'givens.'"

How often we spin our wheels, waste our time, breath, and energy lashing out at what appear to be problems. Look at juvenile delinquency, teen-age pregnancy, illiteracy, and alcoholism! Perceiving these to be *problems*, we compound them by turning to agencies for solutions that haven't a prayer of solving them--because the problems become misstated and erroneously defined the instant they become collective.

"Gang activity up 300 % over ten years, Unwed pregnancy up 15% over the last decade. Twenty percent of this year's high school graduates functionally illiterate. Survey shows 21% of high school seniors get drunk at least monthly." And we wring our hands and moan, "Why doesn't somebody do something?"

Percentage points don't write graffiti, or rob convenience stores; they don't become pregnant or HIV positive; they don't fail reading classes; they don't become alcoholics and drug addicts. Our *kids* do these things, and they do them one kid at a time.

These problems will never--*can* never--be solved with police forces, condom distribution, remedial reading classes, or rehab clinics. But that does not mean there is no solution or hope.

You cannot possibly arrest, convict, and rehabilitate all young punk "wannabe" gangsters in your state, or even in your town. Nor can you patrol every darkened lane or bedroom available to pubescent Romeos and Juliets. You can't teach every child to read. But you can teach *yours* to respect the rights and property of others, and to realize his own self-worth--*if* you accept that it is *your* job, not the police chief's. You can teach chastity, and the wisdom of abstinence, much more effectively than County Services or your clergyman, and *you* can teach them reading skills and love of learning more efficiently than the teachers in any school.

The problem every parent faces, properly stated, is this: "How can I best insure that my child has everything he needs to function as an adult when he leaves the nest?" It is not a question of, "Is the police force adequate?" Or, "Will they remember their condoms?" Or, "Will Ms. Grundy do her job?"

The answer is the same for you as for every other parent in your neighborhood, city, state, and nation. It is, "Quit looking to some impersonal, generic, misfocused *agency* to provide for your child the sense of self, of decency, and responsibility he needs to be truly happy. *Do it yourself*, or it will not get done."

MOTIVATING CHILDREN

While there may be no universally successful method of motivating children, there are some fundamental principles which parents need to be aware of if they intend for their children to follow a course those children may not choose of their own accord.

First is that all children are motivated by *something*. Second, as a parent, you probably know better what motivates *your* child than his kindergarten or first grade teacher will. This is certainly true for the first few months of the school year.

Third is that there are primary and secondary goals, and the desirability of the goal should be the determining factor in selecting a motivator. This is simply a minor spin on the old adage that the end justifies the means.

Not all children respond to gold stars beside their names on a chart, nor are all motivated by the prospect of an A on a report card that may not be seen for nine weeks.

We've never advocated paying kids for good report cards; indeed, had we ever bought into the "$5 per 'A'" game, we would be in debt to our kids until well into the next century. But we do believe that a valid method of motivating children is to *make the desired goal pay off in terms the child understands.* It may not be grades, gold stars, or jelly beans.

Our oldest son began piano lessons at a young age, and progressed well for the first year. Then he discovered baseball. More distressing, he discovered that among the baseball playing set, piano players were not considered "cool." Besides, piano practice cut into ball playing time. We promised him a 10-speed bicycle if he would stick with the piano long enough to master a pre-determined list of pieces. He did it, and he got his bike. That bike was subsequently stolen--but his acquired musical skill was not. Our other son overcame his fear of water and learned to swim for a $30 lock-back knife, which has long since disappeared. But he continues to enjoy the pleasures of swimming.

Our oldest daughter read the Britannica Junior encyclopedia from A to Z during the summer between her 5th and 6th grade year for a $100 bill. She told me once shortly before she graduated from high school (as valedictorian of her class, with a 4.09 g.p.a.) that it had been a rare day, and never a week, without some topic coming up in one class or another with which she had gained familiarity because of that project. She subsequently obtained her bachelor's degree in 3 years and her master's in 4 at Oregon State University--and did it mostly on scholarship funds.

It is worth mentioning that the goals my wife and I had when we got into the par-enting business were not specific in terms of the victories or successes we desired for our children. We didn't set out to create an all-star basketball player, nor successive valedictorians, nor Music-in-May participants, nor scholarship winners. These were goals our children set for themselves. But by the time they achieved them, they had established a history of responding to incentives (call them extortions, bribes, threats, punishments, or whatever you choose) that we as their parents had selected. And they worked.

UNINTENDED LESSONS

In our preoccupation with teaching specific, short-range principles, we are sometimes amazed to find that a lesson of much wider application has been taught. I was discussing parenting experiences and techniques with a co-worker one day when he shared this incident:

"My son had recently married, and I was helping him move. We were carrying a heavy piece of furniture up a ramp into a rented truck. His grip was hampered by a hard, right-angled corner that caused him some distress. He called for me to hold up so he could set it down and get another grip. We were nearly to the top of the ramp, so I urged him just to hurry, since it would have been very difficult for both of us to set the piece down, then pick it back up and resume our trip up the ramp. I explained that there are certain times that operations are easier to complete once started than to interrupt them, and then resume the process. I summarized by saying, 'Son, there are times when you just can't put the load down, even if it hurts.'"

It was some time before the man saw his son again. He learned that the intervening time had been full of conflict and trauma for the son and daughter-in-law. The son had evidently established a pattern of washing out on difficult assignments, so the father voiced his surprise. "Why didn't you just bail out? Lots would have--lots *have*, you know."

The son responded with a wry grin, "Dad, there are times you just can't put the load down, even if it hurts."

Here was an intriguing application of what Dad thought was a purely mechanical, physical principle. How many of the purely physical lessons we try to teach our children will be confirmed down the road in a manner similar to the furniture-moving episode?

1. It is easier to keep your bedroom (or your life) in order than to let it fall into gross disorder and then try to restore it.
2. If you know you are going to be mobile for the foreseeable future, *travel light*.
3. If you are dependent on someone else for a ride, never make him wait on you.
4. *You* are responsible for the return of your own library books, rented videos, or whatever.
5. If you have *sold* your time, it is no longer *your* time.
6. The same ones who decorate for the prom clean up the mess after.
7. Storms are easier to weather if you've battened hatches *before* the wind starts.
8. If you're not the priest assigned, don't steady the ark.
9. A car (or---?) is a handy servant, but a harsh master.

These came quickly to mind. There must be a thousand others.

DATING--WHEN AND WHOM?

As our daughters grew out of the toddler stage, it became obvious to me that the time would come when I would be faced with the problem all fathers face--namely, dealing with unsuitable suitors.

I mapped out a strategy I felt would save me much grief. I would simply lock the daughters in the basement on their 10th birthdays, and let them out on their 21st, at which time they would be free to date whomever they chose, so long as the young man were accompanied by all 4 grandparents. As the oldest approached dating age, I publicized my plan. The looks I received from my daughters inspired a re-examination of my strategy. (I used to have wonderful flashes of inspiration before I had a houseful of teenagers!)

I remembered an experience I had had in 1963. I invited a girl to Homecoming Dance some 4 weeks prior to the big weekend. She was a cheerleader, a very pretty girl, and certain to receive more offers than mine.

She asked how soon I would require an answer. The following Friday night was agreed on. (I later learned that her mother had used the interim time to do some checking up on me through mutual acquaintances.) She consented. I proposed to pick her up around 6:00 o'clock for dinner prior to the 8:00 o'clock dance. She suggested 5:30 would be better.

She met me at the door in blue jeans and a sweatshirt, invited me in, introduced me to her father, and excused herself (to get dressed, I hoped!). I spent the next twenty minutes visiting with her father, unaware that I was being evaluated. It took years for me to realize and appreciate what had happened. But as my daughters approached the time when they would be squired around the countryside by young would-be Romeos, some Daddy's Defense Mechanism dredged this experience up from my memory and persuaded me to look at it in a new light. I decided that this procedure had some merit. I discussed the matter with my wife, and we decided to try the following:

Unless I absolutely knew that a young man was not acceptable, I would be tolerant of choices of escorts to movies, dances, etc., but I would reserve the right to insist that prior to a first date, their friend would have at least one meal at my table, during the course of which I would "read to him from the book." The boy could be advised of the format or not. If he shied away before the meal, good riddance. If the experience itself scared him off, likewise.

Only one young man ever approached me for permission to date one of my daughters. My attempts to rattle him were met with aplomb and candor, and permission was granted. Perhaps the girls' awareness of this threat caused them to be more selective, perhaps today's average young man is several cuts above the norm of my younger years, or perhaps I've just been lucky. At any rate, it is not a bad plan, and better than many. It is certainly better than my first.

DADS & DAUGHTERS

Fathers and daughters have been disagreeing over what constitutes suitable suitors for a long time. The Romeo and Juliet theme did not begin with Shakespeare, and it did not end with "West Side Story," nor is it likely to end as long as daughters continue to attract the attention of young men.

Reasons for these disagreements are many. One is that some young men are less desirable than others, regardless of how desirability is defined, or who defines it. Boy-friends get berated for every conceivable reason. This one rides motorcycles, that one is a rodeo nut. All *this* one thinks about is football, or other sports, *that* one cars. And *that* one, heaven forbid, is into what this generation calls *music!* I have used some of these epithets myself to describe young swains adolescing around my daughters.

Perhaps the syndrome of Daddy/Daughter disagreement stems more from a perspective thing than from analysis of a list of qualifications. I can't speak for all fathers, but I am one. I am also a man who felt the scrutiny of several fathers while attempting to cultivate the affection of their daughters. And as I re-examined (in context, this time) the mood and basis of that scrutiny, and as I examined my own concern, now that it was *my* daughters whose affections were on the line, I discovered new feelings.

There is nothing inherently wrong with motorcycles. Not all who enjoy riding them are Hell's Angels. Rodeos are an outgrowth of a way of life that provides beef to the nation and the world, and I enjoy a steak as much as anybody. Some of the most lucrative incomes paid in this country go to sports figures and musical entertainers, so these can't be dismissed out of hand as being unable to provide for our prized daughters.

So it's not hobbies, interests, or even prospects for careers that concern caring fathers. *It is a fear that whatever that young man's interests, they may be (or may become) more important to them than the happiness of our daughters and grandchildren.*

There are motorcycle buffs for whom bikes are more than a periodic diversion; they are a way of life. For every highly paid athlete, there are countless millions of fans that spend their lives in front of a TV for season after season of repetitive contests, the results of which are seldom remembered past the start of the next season. For every millionaire musician there are countless hundreds struggling for recognition while they spend their evenings in dingy honky-tonks, surrounded by people whose idea of dealing with reality is drowning their discontent in alcohol. There are those for whom otherwise noble interests have displaced family--doctors whose obsession with medicine has destroyed their marriages. There are those whose pursuit of education has become so all-consuming that wife and family have suffered. But in the final analysis, it doesn't make any difference what the young man's interests are. It is simply that they may be more important to him than are our daughters and grandchildren.

We fathers fear that the emotional and physical well-being of our precious daughters could never be as important to a young biker, or musician, or ball player, or even a young doctor as it is to us. So we tend to be hypercritical. It's not because we don't want you to have any fun, girls. It's because we don't want you to ever experience the anguish of having to endure being less important to *him* than you are to *us*.

ASSEMBLY REQUIRED

Among the most exciting acquisitions of childhood are the toys that add to a child's mobility, and thus to his perception of freedom. A tricycle, a ten-speed bike, or that first car--the wherewithal to move faster, farther, and unfettered by parental constraints tends to equate *mobility* with *independence.*

As adolescents respond to the flow of hormones, reach out for heterosexual companionship, and resent the restrictions imposed on them by parents, pastors, and society, they look forward to the institution of marriage as the final--ultimate--vehicle to provide freedom of movement.

Little do they appreciate the preparation that goes into the assembly of those childhood conveyances. How many parents have purchased tricycles, bicycles, and wagons, neglecting to note the small print on the carton: "ASSEMBLY REQUIRED"? It takes considerable mechanical skill to assemble a modern bicycle. Brakes must function properly; sprockets must line up. Ideally, the operator goes through a familiarization course before soloing. That way, if anything goes wrong he or she knows how to fix it.

Many of these expensive toys are used only until something gets out of adjustment. A cable snaps, a wheel gets out of alignment, and the machine is parked and forgotten because the operator lacks the skill, interest, or initiative to make adjustments.

Assembly and orientation processes begin early in one's social career. Even "puppy love" relationships provide opportunities to practice the skills of shifting gears, brake application, signaling for turns, selecting speeds appropriate for existing road and weather conditions, and determining who has right-of-way.

The smooth functioning of a marriage no more begins on a wedding day than the smooth functioning of a ten-speed bicycle begins with the blowing out of birthday candles. It doesn't just happen. *It must be carefully put together by someone who really wants for it to function well.* We can buy the toy, wrap it up in flower-bedecked chapels and catered receptions. But too many realize too late (if ever) that for this or any vehicle to provide a smooth, trouble-free ride, ASSEMBLY IS REQUIRED.

BEHAVIOR & CONSEQUENCES

For a child to function productively as an adult, he must learn at some point that the consequences of unacceptable behavior are unpleasant. Every teacher of my children with whom we met (and than included most of them, at least until they went to college) was told (in the presence of the affected child) that I wanted to know of any misbehavior in the classroom *the day it occurred*, not at report card time or conference time. We would see to it that the misbehavior would not be repeated. The kids evidently lived in fear of our getting a bad report (which was, of course, the whole idea), and conducted themselves properly. By the time they realized that I was not going to crucify them before their classmates they had discovered that appropriate behavior is really the best way to get along. In the 101 "kid-years" (that's 8 kids times 13 school years, minus 3 skipped grades) our children attended public schools, we were *never once* called to bail one of ours out of detention, or the vice-principal's office. We were summoned many times for more pleasant reasons.

One day in the early 1960s 2 a friend of mine and I were out with .22 rifles terrorizing the bird population of the upper Chetco River drainage basin of southwestern Oregon. We killed a bird that had made the mistake of landing in the river within range of our guns. As the volley of shots died away, we heard the shouts of an irate fisherman coming from somewhere down on the river bar. We quickly vacated the area. Around the next bend in the road was Dad's pick-up. The way the brush was cut back from the road made us visible from the river bar, and since my friend's car was the only red Triumph convertible in town, I knew we'd been "made." I told him, "We may as well enjoy ourselves the rest of the afternoon, because when I get home tonight, it'll all be over."

As I came through the living room dragging *Dad's* .22, he looked up from his newspaper. I put the gun away, and returned to face the music. Fortunately for me, Dad had caught a trophy steelhead that afternoon, and was in a better mood than I had a right to expect. It likely saved my life. The ensuing conversation drug out over 30 minutes, counting what drama critics call *pregnant pauses*:

"Was that you up there shooting seagulls awhile ago, Boy?" He knew it was; I knew he knew. Lying would have been futile, as well as counterproductive to my hopes for survival.

"Yes." Pause. "You know that's again' the law, don't you?" "Yes." Pause. "You know what the fine is if they catch you?" "Yes." Pause. "You got that kind of money, Boy?" "No." Pause. "You know where they put you if you can't pay the fine?" "Yes." Pause. "And you know blinkin' well who *ain't* gonna pay the fine?" "Yes."

No pause this time--just a one-eyed squint over what was left of his newspaper, and the most ominous ultimatum I had ever heard. "Just so we understand each other."

I have reflected on this exchange many times over the years, before and since my children began to arrive. He could have threatened by kick my backside, hide the gun, or bend the barrel of it around my neck (and make no mistake, he could have done it), or ground me, or any one of a number of other things. But he knew that if I took a notion to shoot another seagull, I'd find a way. On the other hand--and this is the crux of the matter--I never doubted for an instant that if I got caught, I would have rotted in the local jail before Dad would have sprung dime one for bail. Furthermore, I knew that when the law got done with me, I'd *still* have Dad to reckon with, and those who remember Dad will appreciate that I relished that prospect not at all.

I learned from a good teacher that the consequences of misbehavior are unpleasant. We tried desperately to teach ours the same thing. It's not a bad system. And the principle is the same whether the misbehavior in question is shooting the state's protected birds, or shooting clerks in the state's liquor stores, or "shooting the breeze" at an obnoxious volume in close proximity to others who wish not to be disturbed

It's best that you teach yours *now*, while the acts and consequences are manageable, rather than leaving the task to institutions like reform schools and penitentiaries.

BEHAVIOR & REWARDS

Just as the *consequences* of misbehavior must be communicated to children, so should the concept of *rewards* for good behavior. And there is a delicate line somewhere that each parent must draw and use to accomplish the long-range goals they have set for themselves and their children. At what point is *rewarding* reduced to *bribery*? At what point is threat of *punishment* reduced to *extortion*?

We've already discussed the idea of rewarding kids in terms they understand. While they may not appreciate the advantage of acquiring music skills at age 10, they may be excited about the prospect of a bicycle. By the time the bicycle is stolen, out-grown, or reduced to rust, the skills will (hopefully) have been acquired, honed, and properly valued.

It may be possible to communicate to a child your awareness of the advantages of preparing for college, even while he has ball games to play, video games to master, baseball cards to swap, tapes to dub, and girls to impress or studiously ignore.

You don't have to call it, "Preparing for College." We acquired a collection of books (at garage sale prices) that included a Britannica Junior Encyclopedia. The kids wondered how a set of books like that could possibly be worth the $40 we spent on them, since we were on a very limited budget. Knowing that an idealistic dissertation on the value of reference materials would be wasted, I impulsively decided to make it a matter of dollars and cents. "The skwibb who can read this set, A to Z, between the time school is out in June and resumes in September will be given $200!"

My thinking was that if any of them undertook the project, and stuck with it for even 4 or 5 volumes, they would expose themselves to a wealth of information that would be of value to them in their future studies. They would be productively busy, cheaply entertained, and even modestly informed. Not in my wildest dreams did I expect any of them to take me seriously enough to commit to the project, much less to complete it.

I should have known better than to challenge Heidi on a learning task. She locked herself in a closet with a lamp that summer. She missed completing the reading in the designated time by a week and a half. Understand, I did not have $200. But I was afraid that she would come out of the experience feeling that she had wasted her time. As a consolation we scraped up enough to cash in on a crisp new $100 bill. It seemed like a lot of money to her, and it was to us. Was it worth it? As already mentioned, she graduated with a 4.09 g.p.a. against the heaviest academic load available, and went on to earn a master's degree in 4 years on scholarship monies-- reward for acceptable behavior.

HORIZONS & BOUNDARIES

In Hilton's *Lost Horizon,* two of the main characters discuss the outdated condition of a monastery library located high in the Himalayas. Upon learning that the monastery had no means of communicating with the outside world--nor indeed, any perceived need for such communication--Conway is amazed. "Quite a lot of things have happened in the world since last year," he suggests to his Chinese host. The time is 1930.

Chang's response is worthy of analysis and application to our parenting efforts. He says, "Nothing of importance, my dear sir, that could not have been *foreseen* in 1920, or that will not be *better understood* in 1940."

There are mileposts, plateaus, even crises inherent in every parenting effort, which all but the hopelessly ignorant realize must be dealt with. Children teethe, are weaned, toilet-trained, become verbal, start to school, reach puberty, learn to drive, graduate from high school, and eventually face the prospect of "independence."

These events are all *foreseeable* at conception. Parents know that as surely as the child lives it will pass these mileposts. We need neither newspapers nor pediatric journals to monitor daily progress, nor child behavior specialists post-game quarterbacking in order to improve our prospects for "winning" the next event.

We have the histories of humankind to analyze and put into perspective. *Profiles in Courage,* Plutarch's *Lives,* and similar comparative literary works underscore the similarities in events experienced, and lessons learned by those the world calls "great."

From this and other data we infer:

(1) A broad database of vicarious experiences will enable children to make wiser, more advantageous decisions. Therefore, children who

read *early, avidly,* and *well* are more likely to succeed (however one wishes to define success) than those who learn to read *late,* or who read *reluctantly* and *poorly*--or not at all.

(2) Children who are taught early that the property, space, and sensitivities of others are off limits, and can be violated only with unpleasant consequences to the offender, are less likely to become offenders than those who learn it late. And tragically, those who do not learn it early will likely learn it only upon hearing the judge's gavel fall as sentence is pronounced.

(3) Those who are taught that, "It is *never* okay to hit," are more likely to apply that passive principle to their own behavior (i.e. "Whatever I choose to do will at worst only get me scolded, or sent to my room for a 'time out,' so I'll do as I please") than those who experience therapeutic discomfort for their offensive behavior.

Events studied in retrospect *may well be* better understood later than when current, (as Chang suggested) but they cannot be *changed.* Thus the teachings of a man like Dr. Benjamin Spock can be seen today for the patent absurdities they were decades ago (even by the man who promulgated them) but unfortunately, the effects on the children raised according to them cannot be erased.

As this parent struggled with data pertaining to the preparation of children to recognize and reach for broader horizons, several truisms manifested themselves with ever-increasing clarity. To wit:

(1) Horizons can be reached and stretched only by those who learn and obey the universal laws of travel, and these apply in both literal and figurative senses. Among these are: Don't foul near the water holes; Respect the privacy and rights of others.

(2) Not all who *need* your help know it; not all who know it *want* it; not all who want it *deserve* it; not all who deserve and receive it will respond favorably to it.

(3) How you deal with these attitudes of your fellow travelers will define the limits of your horizons--and the horizons of your children.

RESPECT FOR SPACE & PROPERTY

At some point in time (or more accurately, over a period of time) children must learn to respect the property, space, and sensitivities of others. It starts in the home with parents and siblings, where they learn, "That's *Billy's* ball," or "That's *Mommy's* lipstick, and you are not to bother it." It moves quickly to the neighborhood, and to the belongings and space of others.

Years ago we lived next door to the Halls. One day I was out back chopping wood when Mr. Hall approached me. "Could I have a word with you?" It seems the kids' Frisbee had gotten away from them and gone into Mrs. Hall's strawberry patch. In retrieving it they had not been particularly careful of her plants.

I stopped him and rounded up the children. I lined them up and instructed them to pay close attention to Mr. Hall. "My wife spends a lot of time out here in the garden, and even though we don't get many berries, she takes a lot of pains with them, and enjoys what fruit she gets. She would really appreciate it if you'd be more careful not to damage her strawberries in the future."

"Now, what did he say?" I asked them.

"We don't s'posed to go in the stwawbewies," came the reply.

"Right. That's what he *said*. What it really means is that he is entitled to catch and warm up the next one of you that goes into his garden without an invitation. If your Frisbee or ball goes into his yard, it is *gone*. You may go to their front door and request them to get it for you, but if they're not home, or if they're too busy, or are simply not in the mood to retrieve it, you are out of luck. Understood?" They said they did, and were dismissed.

Mr. Hall had been shaking his head since my line about punishing them himself. "I would NEVER swat one of you kids," he assured me. Fortunately, they were all back in the front yard by this time, and hadn't heard him.

"I honestly don't believe you'll ever have reason to," I assured him. "They don't like spankings, and very seldom receive them. But the reason they don't is because they know that spankings are the mathematically certain result of serious misbehavior. Violating someone's space and damaging his property--even accidentally, and especially after they've been warned--is serious."

This is the way we tried to operate through their young and most impressionable years, and we were consistent enough with this tactic to have seldom been recipients of complaints.

Not violating the space of others includes (besides not tracking through their gardens) not playing music so loud it annoys neighbors. It includes not driving through neighborhoods at excessive speeds. It includes not tormenting friends of younger siblings who happen to be visiting. It includes not walking through the streets of town blazing away with stolen pistols. It even includes such things as being reverent and respectful during worship services, graduation exercises, the playing of the national anthem, and recognizing that the teacher in a classroom has the right to expect them to sit down and be still until he or she is called on.

The results of unacceptable behavior *should* be unpleasant to offenders. And it will be, sooner or later.

REASONS FOR COMPLIANCE

There are three basic reasons for complying with laws and rules. First, it makes our world a more comfortable place to live in. We would all be better off if everyone obeyed traffic laws, property laws, and behavior laws. (Of course, body shops and law enforcement agencies would have to lay off some personnel.) Second, there may be specific benefits. Follow the counsel of a good coach and you'll win more games. Third, the consequences for non-compliance make us uncomfortable. We go directly to jail, without passing "Go."

Both law and life deal with us on all three levels. It appears that the best reason for obedience is that we are all better off for it. In an ideal world, we wouldn't need to be begged, bribed, threatened, or punished to see the advantages of conforming to rules.

Parents bear an obligation to teach their children to obey the laws of the land, the laws of common sense, and the laws of decency. Ideally, all children would understand that it is better not to track through Mrs. Hall's strawberries, or to rip the dress off sister's doll. They would understand the first time it is explained to them, and they would comply. There are even a few children who *do* perform like this, or nearly so. For such as these the tactics of bribery and coercion are not necessary.

This world, however, is far enough from being an ideal place that we have created elaborate systems and theories about how to deal with one another's misbehavior. Some of these systems disagree radically with others. They can be as complex and nonsensical as the methods of Benjamin Spock, or as straightforward and simple as, "Be honest with them, and no baby sitters."

The system we've used has benefited our children, and I list some of the precepts here for consideration. Some will recognize them, and will hopefully forgive me for paraphrasing.

> *No power or influence can or ought to be maintained over children by virtue of parenthood; only by persuasion, long-suffering, and unpretended love.*
>
> *Reprove as necessary--even sharply when called for--afterwards showing an increase of affection towards the reproved, so no bitterness or resentment builds up.*
>
> *Instruct, reward, entice a child--but when you punish a child by whatever means, do it not **because** you are bigger, or **because** you are the parent. Do it because you recognize that he needs to learn conformity and obedience in order to function happily as a citizen.*

All these methods have proven to be effective in many societies, and over many generations. Any parent, or any juvenile guidance counselor who believes *all* children will respond favorably to the, "Now, children, that sort of behavior makes me unhappy," method are doomed to be .200 hitters, and spend their careers at the tail-end of the line up. And the children they work with will seldom get past first base.

Parents who think that the only way to teach compliance is with a belt are not only mistaken, they are criminal. Parents who believe that physical punishment should be the first tactic used are doomed to limited success. Those who believe that no child should *ever* be subjected to therapeutic discomfort take a risk I was never willing to take.

LEARNING FROM CHILDREN

Being human, parents commit errors, misplace priorities, and sometimes forget that we are teaching *children*, not *concepts*. That is to say children are the *subjects*, rather than the *objects* of our teaching efforts. And children, bless their hearts, have the perception and candor to pull the rug out from under our adult wisdom and leave us laughing (or weeping) before the judge and jury or our collective consciences.

Heidi and Holly had missed several days of school with winter complaints. Returning from work one afternoon I met my wife at the door, threw her the car key, and retired to the bathroom. Preparing for my ritual soak, I heard water running through the spigot on the exterior bathroom wall.

I looked out the window to see water being sprayed onto a lawn soaked by days of January rain. I summoned the irrigation crew. They appeared from opposite ends of the house, each clad in T-shirts, jeans, and shower shoes, hoses in hand. I suggested (at some volume) that they turn the water off and return to the living room. I met them there with a lecture about cold weather sickness, appropriate winter outdoor dress, and permission to play in the water. Heidi, tears already flowing, began their defense. "We were just watering the lawn."

I thanked them for their intentions, but explained that lawns on the Oregon Coast don't often need watering in January. Most of my lecture was given to Holly, Heidi having fled to her bedroom. I enlisted Holly's aid in getting the message to Heidi that it was their lack of judgment, not their desire to help that had upset me. Holly joined her sister, and I eavesdropped.

Heidi was wailing. "It's just not fair! We were just trying to help, and we get yelled at! We always get yelled at. Like this morning I was trying to clean the ashes, and Mom said, 'Don't do that, you're making a mess.' So

I got the vacuum to clean it up. It was full, so I tried to empty it and Mom said, 'Don't do that, you're making a mess.' Mom yells at us all day, then goes to the store when Dad gets home, and HE yells at us for watering the lawn, and it's not fair!"

Holly said, "Dad says we don't need to water the lawn in the winter, 'cause it rains."

No good. Heidi returned with, "Know what I think, Holly? I think when it's raining it's 'cause the angels are crying 'cause Dad's being naughty!"

Further exchange resulted in a conspiracy to henceforth retire directly to the bedroom upon arriving home from school, since no matter what they did, it was wrong and got them yelled at, and, "You can't do anything wrong in bed." Holly voiced a concern about getting hungry, but Heidi had a plan to meet that reservation. "We'll just wait till they all go to bed, then raid the fridge."

When Renee returned I explained the gravity of my situation. A simple apology would not extricate me from this; this would involve at least a trip to the Dairy Queen. I made a Dilly Bar run while they were (I hoped!) napping away their anger. Holly came into the kitchen later as Mom . was clearing away the soup bowls, and was sent in before the fireplace to wait while the soup re-heated. I asked her to go invite Heidi to the table, knowing full well that she would not respond to me. As they finished their soup, I got the Dilly Bars from the freezer.

"Know what I've got here?" Tentative nods. "Know who they're for?" More nods, and a guess.

"They're for skwibbs." I qualified their guess.

"Actually, they're for anyone *not* mad at Dad. Do you know anybody that's mad at Dad?" Emphatic nods. "How about you, Holly? Are you mad at Dad?" Barely perceptible negative nod from Holly--daggers from Heidi for selling out. Holly took her Dilly Bar. "How about you, Heidi, are you mad at Dad?" Cold, analytical eyes that seemed to sneer, "Who do you think you're dealing with?" (She'd probably have said, "whom," even that young) and a negative nod which fooled nobody, but got her a Dilly Bar.

"But you said you knew someone who is mad at Dad. Who's mad at Dad?" Big chomp out of her Dilly bar. "You're mad at you'self!"

You seldom fool a child, and never for very long. They will teach you much, if you are willing to learn. About motives, about justice, and about priorities.

QUALITY TIME

Let's talk about the concept of "quality time" in raising children. With so many of today's parents so bent on chasing dollars, golf balls, and other diversions, there needs to be some balm to salve our consciences for not spending adequate *amounts* of time with the children we've sired or borne. The "quality time" myth serves many of us well.

"My husband is gone so much with his job," goes the typical plea, "that he doesn't spend as much time with them as he'd like. But when he's with them, he's *really* with them." Thinking that a week at Disneyland will produce the same results as a half dozen Saturdays at the river or beach is a mistake.

Thinking that a first grade teacher reserving the half-hour between 9:15 and 9:45 for reading instruction each morning will be as effective as your spending similar random blocks of time reading with your child is also a mistake, and for the same basic reason.

Given the size of her classes, and the diversity of backgrounds and attention spans of her charges, Ms. Jones is more or less tied to a curriculum schedule for survival. But (just to illustrate) I have never been a "morning person." It takes me several hours after waking to be approachable with academic challenges. Had I been locked into a 9:00 o'clock reading bloc in first grade, I'd likely never have learned to read. What if your child is similarly afflicted?

If you have taken quarter- or half-hour blocks of time at random (no, not at random, but at your child's request and convenience) for the brief course of his last pre-school summer, and used the time to teach him the alphabet, some basic phonetic combinations, and a few sight words, it won't matter when (or whether) his first grade teacher slots his reading time.

What if the "quality time" you sandwiched in between real estate clients or fishing trips happens to be "off" time for your child? Teaching time, to be most effective, must correspond to a child's "up" times. This is true whether the subject being taught is specifically academic (i.e. times tables or biology) or as nebulous as, "Life in the Marks Family." Teaching is essentially a numbers game, and *it can't be done effectively in isolated, widely separated blocs of time, no matter how "quality" they are.*

I know of no magic formula that prescribes a certain given number of hours of parent/child time required to produce a well-adjusted adult. But simple logic tells me that hundreds of hour-long blocs will be more apt to connect with my child's "up" times, and will produce better bonding and deeper appreciation for my values, than a couple of weeks in each of 8 or 10 consecutive summers in a cabin by the lake.

If you take "time out" for parenting, take it often. Don't limit yourself to 3 or 4 time outs per half, as if you were involved in a basketball game. Parenting is not a game, at least not in the sense of an athletic contest, in which, by definition, there is a winner and a loser. We're not *competing* with our children. Either we both *win*, or we both *lose*. Let's be winners.

Imagine the absurdity of a farmer agonizing over his crop failure wailing, "Granted, I didn't irrigate my fields as often as I'd have liked, but when I did, I really soaked them." Quality crops are not grown that way. And neither are quality kids.

COST & VALUE

Most parents profess to want what is best for their children. The baby-boom population in this country is primarily a product of post-Great Depression parents. In many cases both parents worked during the developmental years of their children, "So they could have the things we did without."

"I gave them everything money could buy," is an alibi often used by parents disclaiming responsibility for the aberrant behavior of their teenagers. Could it be that the most important things we can give our children cannot be *bought*? Could it even be that the very pursuit of (and bestowal of) dollars and what they will buy can keep us from giving our children what they need most? Yes and yes.

I remember the first boy in my class to have his own car. It was brand new, and a gift from an indulgent guardian. He was active in class politics, as well as sports and music, and was well-liked. By our senior year, he had dropped participation in sports and music, held no class or student-body office--in fact was involved in no activities except week-end parties at which he began the trip into alcoholism. His grades prevented him from graduating with us. The last time I saw him he was married to his fourth wife.

I remember another boy whose father had provided a fund for his college education. He partied the money away, dropped out of college and entered military service. He later returned with his own savings and the G.I. bill, cleaned up his academic record, and eventually graduated as a licensed professional.

What is a car--or an education--worth? It would presumptuous of me to claim that the gift of that car is what ruined my friend's chances for happiness as an adult, or that the other's education assured him a productive and fulfilling career. But I do believe that the relative *worth* of these acquisitions (or any other, for that matter) is determined by *what they cost the recipient in terms of personal effort.*

By lavishing on our children everything money can buy, we run the real risk of communicating to them that they are *entitled* to the finer things of life for no other reason than they happen to be ours. I'll not bother arguing whether or not happiness, fulfillment, and contentment are correlated to *things* (fine, or any other kind). Supermarket tabloids chronicling "Divorce Proceedings of the Rich and Famous," do that more eloquently than I ever could.

Children (even young ones) value those toys and clothes most that they have purchased with their own money. Any parent can confirm this. Whether that money is accumulated allowance, proceeds from berries picked and sold, or neighbors' lawns mowed is irrelevant. *They value most what cost them most in terms of personal investment.*

If a college education (or a car, or anything else) is to have any *lasting* value, it is worth the effort required to obtain it. Whatever we give our children, whatever we teach them--if we have neglected to instill in them the awareness that **value is determined by personal investment**, we have done them a disservice.

PREPARATIONS FOR PARENTHOOD

Ask a typical class of high school sophomores or juniors to define "family," and you get a tragic commentary on our times. In my daughter's Family Living class of 18 students she was the only one who said, "A husband, his wife, and their children." She was also the only one of the 18 whose family circumstances were thus described. Other definitions included: Half- or step-siblings, step-parents, mom's live-in boyfriend, and variations of these. The gap between "ideal" and "normal" is wide.

It is unthinkable that this gap is being deliberately caused; that people enter marriage with a pre-formed plan to struggle with custody battles and divorce settlements. Surely something can be done to improve chances for success--success being defined as a *permanent* union between a husband and wife, and a dual-biological parent atmosphere in which children can grow and mature.

Forget applying this hope to broad national charts, and apply the question individually. Can *you* do anything that will decrease *your* chances of becoming another percentage point on a divorce statistic chart? Is there some program *you* can begin that will insulate *your* children from the emotional trauma of seeing the two people they love most in this world scalding one another with verbal venom while jockeying for possession of toys, furniture, and living souls? And if the answer is, "Yes!" to whom can we turn for direction and counsel? To advice columnists?

Ann Landers had been handing out counsel on every subject imaginable for decades upon the dissolution of her marriage when she commented, "The lady with all the answers doesn't have all the answers. Chalk it up as another marriage that didn't make it to the finish line."

I once discussed with a former high school friend our respective states of marital contentment. I had been married about 3 years at the time, having married at age 27. He was married to his third wife, from whom he was subsequently divorced. The last time I saw him he was married to wife number 4. I mentioned my satisfaction with my first and only, and that the wait had been worth it, and that I could hardly have done better had I taken another 27 years in searching. He said, "Experience is the best teacher." Maybe.

But for me, *best* means, "whatever hurts the least." I have never enjoyed pain, be it physical, emotional, or psychological. I prefer "economy of pain." I used some tactics and techniques in my mate selection process that served me well. I am pleased enough with my success to presume that they are worth sharing.

Remember that human personalities are varied and varying, and that where human relationships are concerned, *nothing* is absolutely certain. So we play percentages, try to improve our chances for success, just as Ted Williams did when he studied pitchers. We study what has worked, what hasn't worked, and remind ourselves that if it is true that experience is a good teacher, it is also true that we don't have to make all the mistakes *ourselves*--we can learn from the mistakes of others.

We'll begin by making some statements that appear to me to be truisms, and not subject to debate.

1. To have the *best* chance at raising good kids, you must be a good parent.
2. To be the *best parent*, you must both *have* and *be* a good spouse.
3. To be *most* successful as a spouse, you must be a successful *spouse selector*.

How to select to best advantage the best "other parent" for your children? (Before we proceed, let me warn the Harlequin Romance fans that what I am about to suggest will probably challenge--maybe even *offend*--their concept of true love.)

Make a physical list of what you hope to find in your ideal mate. Include the traits you consider to be desirable, first in your ideal *partner*, then in what you consider to be the ideal *other* parent for your children. Don't worry about prioritizing the list yet. You will want to let it gel for a while and rewrite it anyway, adding, deleting, and rearranging as your reflecting, pondering, and findings dictate.

Next make a list of all the successful parents you know of with whom you are personally acquainted. Below each name include what you perceive to be the traits and practices that *made* them successful. Talk to them, if they are available. Ask them specific questions regarding their success. Now revise your first list, and prioritize it based on your findings.

Next, list all the unsuccessful (or less successful) parents you know, complete with what you sense are the contributing factors to their *lack* of success. Interviewing this group may not be politically prudent; it may be safest to trust your own judgment. Now, revise your first list again, incorporating your new data.

By now you will likely have a "wish list" that includes (in some order or other) requirements in personality, sense of humor, interests, sex appeal, politics, theology, attitudes--towards your own gender, family, children, and much else.

Now it gets sticky. If you have a current love interest to whom you are more or less committed--ask yourself, "How does he or she measure up to this list?" If you don't get a 90-95% match, you should consider bailing out of this thing *right now*, while you can cut your losses, and look elsewhere. Please, *please, **please*** don't fall victim to the illusion that because he or she *claims* to love you that that will *negate* those differences. The odds are against it. (Don't take my word for this--just look around! I once had a co-worker insist that, "Love conquers all!" I surveyed 4 others in the room, and established that of the 6 of us, my co-worker and I were the only ones who had been married only once. The others conceded that when those first marriages failed, it proved to them that love does NOT, in fact, conquer all. We didn't even have to leave the *room* to demonstrate the fallacy of that piece of folk wisdom.)

Next, (and this requires even more brutal honesty and soul-searching) assuming your candidate matches favorably to your list, ask yourself, "Why should he or she be willing to 'forsake all others' for a chance to throw in with me?"

The best advice I ever got on this subject was from a high school counselor several years after my graduation and several more prior to meeting my wife. It fell into two related areas. Having established that I did, in fact, have some sort of list in mind she said, *"Don't let your search for perfection blind you to excellence."* Then she added, *"You worry about becoming the kind of man your ideal girl is looking for."*

To her gem of wisdom I add an observation of my own, gleaned from years of study: *"Don't let having identified excellence blind you to fatal flaws."* There are many excellent (but imperfect) human beings in the world, and most of them will make good mates for someone. Not all of them are suitable for you.

METHODS & PUBLIC OPINION

In the early '60's, Oregon State University produced an all-American quarterback named Terry Baker. This was before the days of interminable play-offs, Super Bowls, and BCS games, so it was the custom to pit each season's college all-stars against the NFL champions to give the scouts a chance to see how the college boys performed against professional talent.

Otto Graham coached the college all-stars that year, and elected to go with a quarterback named Ron Van DerKellen (who, if my memory serves me correctly, was from Wisconsin). The all-stars beat that year's NFL champion Green Bay Packers. Graham took some heat from the western sports writers for leaving Baker on the bench. His defense was simple and eloquent. "My job was to beat Green Bay. I beat Green Bay."

My wife and I often faced criticism of neighbors, friends, school officials, and even family members for methods we used, and lessons we taught preparing our children for life outside the home and classroom. We were faulted by well-meaning acquaintances for disposing of our television when our oldest child was barely 6 years old. Even my own mother protested. The kids themselves squalled for a couple of Saturdays, until they had successfully weathered the cold turkey of cartoon withdrawal.

Our job, as we perceived it, was to prepare the children for the artificially competitive environment of public schoolrooms. It appeared to us that the most crucial *tools* for success during this 13-year term were the desire and ability to *read*. We bought books, got library cards, and taught our children to read. Five of our 8 children have bachelor's degrees, 2 have master's, and one of these a Ph.D. It appears we were correct in our assessment. Our children have done well, not only in school, but in sports, fine arts, and in the job market.

We were criticized for depriving our kids of Sesame Street, Mr. Rogers, Wild Kingdom, National Geographic specials, and many other valuable and interesting programs. We were guilty. But we also deprived them of thousands of hours of exposure to violence, seamy sex, and tasteless, inane sitcoms,. During these hours of "deprivation" we joined them as they sailed with Jim Hawkins to *Treasure Island*, and floated down the Mississippi with Huck Finn, and rode trails of the American southwest with the Sacketts and other Louis L'Amour heroes.

I taught my son how to defend himself against playground bullies--*bully*, actually, since it was only necessary to use this skill once in his public school career. After he reached an understanding with that one, the others never bothered him. Interestingly, they never bothered any of his friends either, as long as he was near. I was accused of advocating violence, and was warned that my son would take the instruction I had given him as license to wreak havoc on the weak and timid; that he would become a perpetual problem to myself and school principals. It never happened--mostly because we had taught him during those reading sessions, and through other family activities, that bullies are not appreciated. Acceptable times to hit are determined by long-established rules of propriety, not by individual tempers, moods, and selfish opportunism.

To those who fault us for not using *their* rulebook or game plan to train our children: Our job was to equip them to perform in the school system, the athletic arena, and the adult world. To paraphrase Otto Graham, our job was help our children beat the averages within the confines of the rules. We've done that.

GOOD KIDS

We have a policy in American society of recognizing top achievers among our youth. At spelling bees, winners are given congratulations and dictionaries; at awards assemblies star athletes are given medallions and pins for letter-jackets; at graduation ceremonies scholarships are given to top scholars, and valedictorians address us.

Following up on these top performers is sometimes a disappointment. Ten years out of high school we find high school standouts who fail to make the grade in college; many all-conference athletes at the high school level never participate in anything more demanding than viewing the Super Bowl game following graduation. Their marriages fail at the same or higher rates than those of their classmates whose performances attracted no attention, and their contributions in other areas often fall short of our expectations.

On the other hand, those whose performances failed to draw accolades often surprise us. There seems to be little correlation between what high school students consider "cool" and the disposition to succeed in the adult world. Is there an indicator--an identifying trait or behavior pattern that is an *accurate* predictor of adult success? In short, what does it take to qualify as a "good kid"? My personal experience and observation of kids has led me to formulate some generalizations we list here for what they may be worth.

A "good kid" does not have to be a champion *every*thing or even a champion *any*thing. He need not even be an above average performer. He must, however, have learned (or be in the process of learning) to respect the space, sensitivities, and property of others.

How often we see gifted athletes assume the role of Casanovas, playing with the hearts of their admirers with no concern for the virtue of their victims, or the paternity of their victims' children. One need only walk through a mall, or spread a picnic lunch on the beach or river bar to be reminded of how few of our youth have any appreciation for the space and sensitivity of others. "Boomboxes" and car stereos fill the air with obnox-ious racket, making it impossible to converse with those sharing our blanket. To request that they turn it down is to invite a barrage of profane suggestions. "Good kids" don't behave like this, regardless of their academic standing or athletic prowess. They don't leave behind them pyramids of beer and soda cans, or piles of assorted picnic debris. Good kids are aware of others, and are considerate of their sensitivities.

Good kids know that there are things more important in life than their own perpetual entertainment. They will be seen having fun, of course. But they will also be seen bagging groceries, waiting counters, and picking fruit. They'll be seen washing cars for someone else's benefit, and mowing lawns for widows, and singing Christmas carols in rest homes while delivering holiday treats they baked themselves. They'll baby-sit, chop wood, and rake leaves, and they'll be proud of the clothes and toys they buy with the money thus earned. They'll even spend some of that money on Mother's Day presents, and taking younger siblings to Saturday matinees.

They have learned, or are learning, that nothing of lasting worth will ever come to them (except the love and closeness they share with family and chosen loved ones) through any other means than their individual efforts.

NATURAL SELECTION--AND
ARRIVAL OF THE FITTEST

There comes a time in the life of every boy when he becomes aware of a particular girl, separate and apart from the nebulous masses of "GIRLS!"--when he recognizes that there is something about *this* one that bears scrutiny, and for whom forgiveness for *not* being a boy might be in order.

For me the moment came in the fifth grade. Her name was Dixie, and she was beautiful. She was in fourth grade and so sat across the room (a split 4th/5th grade class) a seat or two ahead of me so I had a view of her from three-quarter profile--perfect, since she couldn't see me staring at her unless she happened to look back over her right shoulder.

There had been girls that I acknowledged were prettier than others, but I saw no reason to attach any significance to the assessment. Some *cars* I found prettier than others, too--so what? But for reasons that would later be explained to me in health and biology classes, I saw something in Dixie that not only compelled my gaze to keep returning, but inspired me to find a method of attracting her attention.

The playground swings were just outside our classroom door. One day I was swinging at maximum altitude when Dixie took the swing next to mine. One method we boys had developed to exhibit our machismo was to spin our swings while swinging at maximum height. The prudent would only do this in the center swings, where chain length would prevent the daredevil from making contact with the A-frame that supported the swings.

Two things were working against me that day. First, I was in an outside swing. Second, my urgency to be noticed by Dixie was borderline terminal. I started into my spin at the bottom of the arc, and by the time I had peaked, was totally out of control. During the return to nadir I crashed into the A-frame with the back of my head, causing the pipe to produce (at substantial volume) an A-flat below middle C.

I never knew whether Dixie noticed me--my concerns were in other areas for awhile. By the time the stars had dimmed and the goose egg had receded, I had concluded that even if she *had* noticed me, the price was too high. I don't believe I ever had another class with her, though we attended the same school until I graduated. By the time I had regained interest in attracting her attention, she had grown about 8 inches and I only 2. By the time I had gained sufficient stature to have stood a chance with her, I was off seeing the world.

Next to attract my serious attention was Judy. I was in 8th grade, she in 7th. Word had come to me through the corridor grapevine that she thought I was cute. I had been trying to screw up courage to ask a girl to one of our monthly junior high dances, but fear of rejection had quelled the urge. But here was hope! If I were to ask Judy, and she already thought I was cute--I let it all hang out. She accepted! We went to several dances over the next couple of years, some school functions, some sponsored by the Rainbow Girls. Gradually the elation of not being rejected cooled. She was cute enough to attract the attention of guys more committed to pursuit--she realized there were others more desirable--who knows why it went the way of most adolescent romances?

During, and for some time after my fascination with Judy, there were other girls around me of whom I was aware. Some were neighbors--Linda, Marlene, Karen, and/or friends of my sister--Carolyn, Kathy, another Linda. Mostly these were targets of my abuse and disdain, though many of them were nice enough girls. Certainly all of them deserved more respect and courtesy than I gave them. But by this time my two oldest sisters had attracted lines of admirers, and with them a compulsion for soap-opera scenarios that left me tired and disgusted. My unverbalized position was, "If part and parcel of the boy/girl thing is tears and trauma, I'd rather pass."

My senior year I only remember dating 4 girls. First was Carol (who was a freshman). I had been talked into this unfortunate situation against my better judgment by 2 senior girls. Second was Peggy, a new girl from Colorado who asked me to a Sadie Hawkins dance. Third was Joanne, who broke off an engagement a couple of months before graduation so she could spend enough time with me to put her commitment to her fiancé into perspective. Actually, I don't remember that we dated, though we marched together at graduation and did spend some time together. Last was Mary, daughter of a friend of Dad's, with whom I had corresponded for some time. I attended her graduation ceremony and party, and basically never went back.

The year following graduation I dated only 4 girls, each only once. Yvonne, whose parents gave me a couple of planks in my own parenting platform; Janet, who had been the flame of a now absent buddy; Marianne, whose boyfriend (my best buddy) was attending the Naval Academy (I took her to her senior prom); and finally Carolyn, whom I took to a movie. (Following the movie we went to a drive-in restaurant where I was waited on by the most beautiful blue-eyed redhead--bar none--I have ever seen.)

During my mission and military service, my preoccupation with girls was a decidedly "back-burner" proposition. As a missionary I had agreed to keep girls "at arm's length," both figuratively and literally. While in the Army, my position was that I'd not pursue the matter of pursuit, since close association with G.I.s quickly convinced me that girls attracted to soldiers presented special dangers.

I did, however, have some contact with "eligibles." One was Helga, a contact I had taught as a missionary, and with whom I had corresponded later. I extended my tour of duty in Viet Nam for 6 months for the opportunity to return to Germany to explore possibilities. It was quickly evident that there was nothing there.

In numerous trips to Hameln during my last year of military service I met perhaps 6 or 8 lady missionaries, some of whom could have been considered possibilities--except for the fact that *they* were missionaries, and by definition off limits, as I was to them.

It is only right to mention here two women who had a profound impact on my life in general, and on my search for a wife specifically. One was my high school counselor, who gave me advice (already mentioned) for Galahads in pursuit of an ideal damsel. She said, *"Don't let your search for perfection blind you to excellence."* I never considered a girl after that without recalling this counsel, and upon rejecting some highly favored ones, I did some agonizing over whether the rejections were for lack of perfection, or for insufficient excellence.

The other was Mutti (German for "Mom"), my landlady for 10 months in the Pied Piper city of Hameln. I discussed with her many facets of love and life. She nursed me through a month of the worst illness of my life, with all the genuine care and concern any mother ever showed her own child. From her--no, *with* her--I learned of love that is not limited to blood ties, nor by biological attractions, nor ideological compatibility, nor upon any of the principles which previous associations had been based.

Her concern for my successful pairing was at once touching and entertaining. Those in whom I exhibited the slightest interest, but whom she found unacceptable, she was free and comical with put-downs. Those she considered real possibilities would have their qualities paraded before me in a manner to rival a Miss America pageant. Realizing that it wouldn't be proper for me to attempt to curry the favor of a currently serving lady missionary, she would say, "But such a one you should find."

Out of the Army, into BYU, and the hunt was seriously on. I never pretended that I went to Utah for educational purposes, though I didn't resent the class time I logged over the next year. There was Susan ("Anyone that cute, that smart, that wealthy, and that old--and still single? *There's a barb somewhere*," Mutti insisted.) Then, Ann (former missionary and now free to acquire whatever set of headaches she preferred.) "Subconsciously, I'd still wish for you Ann," Mutti once confided. Dad and I both wondered how she would have phrased this wish had she ever given it *conscious* thought.

Then there was Renee, another former missionary Mutti had known after my stint in Hameln. Mutti tried to engineer a meeting for us during the summer of 1970 that didn't come off. When I explained to her that my heart was not broken because this meeting failed to take place--that my heart didn't need *repair* but only, perhaps, some *renovation*, she replied, "Not renovation--*Renee*-vation!"

She was right. My conclusion that Renee was the one I was looking for did not stem from, nor was it dependent on Mutti's decree. She knew the part of me that was lacking, and that Renee would plant, nurture, and bring to fruition. The search was over. It was worth the wait.

ON PARDONS AND GARDENS

We've all heard the optimist/pessimist thing, where one sees the roses, another the thorns, or the glass is either half empty or half full. There is more involved than mere attitudes or moods. What is perceived and interpreted by one's senses is determined by the *sum of the experiences the observer has had.* A person who has ridden his bicycle through a rose trellis can't be faulted for being more cognizant of thorns than blossoms.

For most of my adult life I've been exposed to men who felt compelled to discuss with co-workers their domestic situations. I've heard women praised and berated, cursed and lauded. I've heard them referred to in flattering metaphor and the most disparaging language, and I wondered from an early age how perceptions could vary so dramatically.

The first time I remember consciously gathering data for future reference in this arena was in Celle, Germany, in 1966. I was at a church activity night, and volleyball was the event. A young married couple had been chosen by opposing team captains. Helga declined, saying, "Gegen mein Mann spiele ich nicht." (Against my husband, I do not compete.) My acquaintance with this couple, though brief, allowed me to assess this statement. I didn't perceive a subservient, subjugated, brow-beaten second-class citizen who had no identity apart from being Frau Paul. I sensed an attitude of commitment *to,* and co-operation *with* her chosen partner, that went way beyond sharing of living quarters, meals, and surname. I saw a oneness, an "us-ness," a "we don't compete even in fun; we are a team"-ness. I decided I wanted that.

Within a year I was in the Army, surrounded by scores of primarily young men, many of whom were married or engaged. I had frequent occasion to hear them discourse on the nature of their relationships. I listened closely for the signs of partnership and co-operative interest I had observed with the Paul's. When I found it, I made a point of getting well enough acquainted with the subjects to question them about the techniques and methods they had used to achieve it.

When I sensed negative elements, I often asked the complainers what had caused their dissatisfaction, since obviously at some point the women they were criticizing must have seemed to them worthy of more positive comment. I developed from their responses a database of tactics and attitudes to avoid if I hoped to someday experience a high level of marital bliss.

I've heard disgruntled husbands refer to their wives as, "my ball and chain," "a tough row to hoe," "the old lady," and other terms considerably less flattering. Not having shared their experiences, it is not for me to state how accurately these appellations might describe the women they chose. But by examining the metaphors, and by factoring in some observations of men in general and *complaining* men in particular, I can make some inferences that might benefit the young and as yet uncommitted seeker.

To a man whose posture is, "It's my divine right to spend one night a week bowling and drinking beer with my buddies, or X number of hours a week parked in front of a TV watching ballgames" (or fill in here any of the life styles of the men you've heard bemoan their lots in life as prison sentences), a woman who takes exception could well *seem* like the ball and chain once shackled to the legs of convicted felons.

To a man who is met with criticism no matter what his income, hobbies, or interests might be, a harping, sniping, complaining woman could well be a "tough row to hoe." And "old lady," (spoken as one word) does seem to describe a lot of women, even some who have not reached middle age. *It doesn't have to be that way.*

I was placed in circumstances that effectively prevented my making my mate selection until my late twenties. By then I had figured out some of the things I wanted married life to provide me *with*--and I knew some of the things bachelorhood deprived me *of*, that I wanted very much to change. So when I left the Army and re-entered the real world (read: wife-quest), I had some solid ideas about what I was looking for, and looking to avoid, and at least some of the things I needed to do to make it happen.

For example, I like kids, and I was frustrated by having to, in effect, borrow them from my friends and relatives. I wanted my own to come home to, to romp with, to tease, to teach, love, and enjoy. A proper wife would provide them. I was tired of eating my meals at a table with dozens of coarse, unpolished, profane men, whose mutual interests focused on incontinence, intemperance, and sensuality. A proper mate would provide me with congenial dinner conversation.

I was lonely--tired of planning alone, hoping alone, praying alone, and sleeping alone. A proper partner would fill these voids. So I conducted my search and made my selection based on these experiences and aspirations.

When I reflect on my marital status, and when the subject arises on the job, or in any conversation whatsoever, I make no reference to a ball and chain. I see Renee as a Pardon--a release from the confinements and voids I had grown so weary of as a single man. I sympathize with those who feel they have a "tough row to hoe," but I perceive my choice as a Garden--a veritable Eden of fruits and flowers, the savoring of which has never bored nor disappointed me, nor ever caused me to covet another man's husbandry nor his husbandhood.

"Old lady?" Well, I suppose old is relative. She's weathered 7 decades now, 4+ of them in harness with me, so let those call her old who view her from the sub-twenty portion of the population. But, "Lady"? Oh, yes--in the purest, most reverent, and undiluted sense of the word.

"They Twain Shall Be One"

She's a thing I see, but more--the Way I see things--
A song I hear, but more--the Way I Sing.
A warm idea lingering in my mind--
But more a Way of Thought.
Not a ball and chain, but more a Pardon;
More a Way of gardening than a garden.
Awaited Fruit that promised in the flower--
Less a prize I've won, but more--a Power--
A Power of Purchase, not a trinket bought.
We twain are one--That God should be so kind!

CREDIT WHERE CREDIT IS DUE

I often hear, "Sure, it's nice if your children read, and it helps if they've learned how to behave, and there is no question that things go smoother when they respond to your efforts to bribe, persuade, or intimidate them--but what's the bottom line? To what single thing do you give most credit for the success your now adult children enjoy?"

It is fitting and proper to respond to this question. The answer to the question, "Where do those all-star kids come from?" is simply, "From an all-star mother."

All-star mothers don't *compete* for recognition as do athletes, scholarship applicants, or Jeopardy contestants. No one keeps score. No one times their laundry cycles, or tallies miles driven to and from music lessons and ball practice; no one compares shopping lists to determine who leads the league in coupon redemption. But Supermoms *are* super, lack of tally sheets notwithstanding. And how do we determine who is a World-class Mom? May I suggest the standard Jesus used to measure the validity of prophetic callings: *"By their fruits ye shall know them."*

Listing the achievements of her children offends her. She finds it immodest. Okay. Suffice it to say that clearly, this mother has done something right. To put the magnitude of her performance into perspective, consider: Her 8 children were born in the 12 years between 1972 and 1984, long after the advent of the Pill. In an era when many women over 30 have gone through 2 or 3 husbands, she stayed with the one she began with. At a time when many women were having their tubes tied, or their husbands vasectomized following the birth of their second babies, she continued to endure the discomfort, the discomfiture--and the unspeakable joy--of bringing them into the world. When most women with her occupational skills had achieved a level that would allow them to hire housekeeping chores done, and their kids tended, she for some years held down a 40-hour a week job, cooked, laundered, and shopped for her own, and *was* and *is* bewildered when anyone feels she has done anything remarkable.

To illustrate the depth of her commitment to her domestic situation: Once the sawmill crew I worked with stole some of her cookies out of my lunchbox. They were so impressed with the quality of them that they smuggled a note into the box extending a fabulous offer. If she would divorce me, they would agree to support her and the children, and would ask nothing in return but that she keep them supplied with snickerdoodles--and she turned them down!

If such a mother is the main reason for the performance of our children, perhaps my providing a list of parenting do's and don't's is a study in busy work. If you are a father whose kids are already teen-agers, it is a bit late to consider whom you would prefer for their mother, though if you are a mother who feels deficient in Supermom skills, it is never too late to set about acquiring them.

So, it would appear that Renee should be supplying this commentary, and not I. And the target group that would stand to benefit most from a study of her methods and tactics would be women and girls who have yet to become mothers, but want to become good ones, and men and boys who want to find such a woman for the mother of their own children.

Would God that the entire next generation be so fortunate!

ON IN-LAWS

In the preceding chapter we noted that he who sets for himself the goal of raising quality children does well to select for their mother a quality wife. That is too understated: **Whatever hope a man has of producing quality children will be realized _proportionally_ to the quality of the woman he selects to be their mother.**

Once during a visit with my mother-in-law we discussed the hope of someday publishing these musings. The two of us had delighted in kidding and needling each other for the duration of our acquaintance. Let it be understood that I have always held her in highest regard and have never been able to relate to mother-in-law jokes and diatribe so prevalent in our culture and lore. I don't doubt that there _are_ mothers-in-law who are justly detested and resented by the spouses of their children--I've simply had the good fortune not to have experienced one.

She jokingly asked when I would do a piece on mothers-in-law. I realized immediately that this collection could not be complete without it. There is no doubt that your child's "other" grandma will contribute to your chances of successfully rearing quality children--and this contribution will go far beyond the gene pool.

Has she raised your mate to be self-reliant? Has she raised him or her to come running to _her_ for solutions to every little problem? Has she shown that those deeply personal concerns your spouse discusses with her will be held in sacred trust, or does she deal with them as though they were public domain, and worthy of being rehashed with the rest of the extended family?

Having raised your spouse, does she see it as her divine right to foist her experience onto _your_ stewardship unsolicited? No doubt young parents *can* and *should* learn much from seasoned veterans, but things learned in *compulsory* classes are often resented--and seldom treasured.

Does she show noticeable favoritism towards your spouse or one of his or her siblings? If yes, your partner will reflect the negative effects of this, including having a favorite among *your* children, thus creating the potential for the sort of sibling rivalry that destroys family solidarity and fosters generations of bitterness and resentment.

How does she regard and refer to her own husband? If she has not developed a husband/wife relationship that she treasures, it is unlikely that she will treasure *yours*--and her meddling, prying--even commenting--will become a source of contention.

If you have *already* made your mate selection, this commentary is too late to help you much. But if you are still in the "search" mode, any effort invested in getting a handle on your future mother-in-law's demeanor and disposition will be energy well spent. (To avoid the charge of chauvinism, the same profile needs to be applied to fathers-in-law.)

I had often made the comment prior to my own wedding that when I got married, it would be to a *wife*, not to a tribe of in-laws. By the time I realized the absurdity of this position, I had already married into as fine a family of in-laws as exists on the planet.

The healthy and wholesome facets of "mother-in-lawhood" manifest themselves during the courting process. Be aware of them--draw them out. Discuss topics with the siblings of your future spouse that will provide insight. If the data thus gained paints a bleak picture you have 3 choices:

(1) *Bail out now, and cut your losses, or*

(2) *Marry him or her and move to the dark side of the moon. I'm not talking about upstate, or to a neighboring state--I'm thinking New Zealand, or Capetown--and don't have a telephone or mailing address for the first 3 years, or*

(3) *Get yourself a good saddle, because you'll be in for a long, difficult ride.*

In-laws--especially mothers-in-law--can be either a tremendous asset or a heavy burden in your effort to provide a wholesome environment for your children. She is part of the package. May all who take their parenting seriously be as fortunate as I have been.

TELEVISION: NEMESIS OF READING

Over the last score or more of years, we have taught a number of seminars designed to help parents teach their pre-school children to read. We always stress that the chances for success with our program are inversely proportional to the accessibility of television. We are usually challenged on this point, and have it pointed out to us that there are many programs worth watching. We realize this. Our denunciation of television has more to do with *accessibility* than with programming, and with its ability to simply interfere with more worthwhile endeavors.

Through the avenue of television I watched the first man set foot on the moon; I watched Mt. Saint Helen erupt; I watched Jack Ruby shoot Lee Oswald; I watched Hank Aaron break Babe Ruth's home run record. A dozen or more times I've watched a video showing my own son set the single-season scoring record for his high school basketball team. Of course television has value.

The problem with it, especially for aspiring pre-school readers, is that it simply gets in the way. It reduces the opportunity--and even the reason--for them to use their imaginations. But we can't ignore the fact that so much of what they see, both in the programming and in the commercials, is mindless drivel devoid of any positive attribute.

When my wife was in the hospital with our 4th child, my oldest son and I watched a detective show that portrayed the infiltration, arrest, and sentencing of a baby-stealing ring. He instantly developed a fear that someone would steal his new sister. I chucked the TV the next day. I was accused of overreacting--of mishandling the episode. Maybe. I was also accused of depriving them of a host of wholesome, informative, and edifying material. Maybe. But I also kept them separated from countless hours of mindless sitcom fare whose tasteless storylines put a premium on smart-mouthed, superficial, flippant children whose salient characteristic is disrespect for authority.

Many of those hours we were "depriving" them of access to that sort of garbage, we spent with them enjoying quality literature and one another's company. We--and *they*--read biographies of American and world leaders, National Geographic, scriptures, encyclopedias, and whatever else tickled their eclectic fancies. They read the Hardy Boys, Nancy Drew--and they got Laura Ingalls Wilder from *Laura*, not Michael Landon.

One of them asked me during our TV-less period, "Dad, how do we *imagine*? I mean, when the Hardy Boys are sneaking up a mountain trail, and this cougar is creeping out on a limb, waiting in a tree, you can just... well, you know...How do we do that?"

I could only tell him, "I'm not sure. But it is an *acquired* skill, and it gets better with practice. And you don't get much practice at it sitting comatose in front of a TV."

For us, and I fear for most families, rationing or being selective with TV viewing is virtually impossible. Cold turkey only caused us difficulty for 2 or 3 cartoonless Saturdays; then reading took over. And just look at how our children have suffered.

PURPOSE & PERSPECTIVE

The focus of one's efforts invested in any undertaking will be determined largely by what the finished product is intended to be or represent. The care a young 4H-er gives a head of livestock intended to be Grand Champion and next year's fair is understandably intense and personal. The attention a rancher gives a newborn calf or lamb that comprises a hundredth part of his spring crop tends to be general and generic.

An adult who has owned a dozen or more automobiles is apt to view his current vehicle (even if brand new) as a *ride*, a *tool* designed to move him from Point A to Point B with whatever level of efficiency, luxury, and practicality he feels comfortable. A teen-age owner of his first car is likely to view it as a manifestation (or at least an extension) of his personality. He will often spend hard-earned dollars on sporty accessories, sound systems, trick lights, or custom paint. For such a driver cost-per-mile is not a factor. Fuel efficiency, practicality, and serviceability are not considerations. Looks, horsepower, and vintage will be more important. But whatever the tastes of the owners, cars are relatively short-lived, and their passing from our ownership is easily adjusted to.

What about the acquisition of children? Do we acquire them simply as a result of satisfying natural urges? Do we need the extra hands to harvest our crops? Do they appear as unwanted results of our indiscretions--our sexual irresponsibility?

Certainly children have been born for all these reasons, and for others more and less noble. And the effort their parents expend on them is going to reflect their basic perception of what children are all about. Children born as a result of recklessness, or wantonness are apt to be viewed by their parents (or more often just the mother, since the father responsible--make that *irresponsible*--has deserted them) as nuisances. Training, encouragement, and motivation in the areas of education and social responsibility will often be woefully inadequate or misfocused. Sadly, the wrecking yards, and even the highways of society, are filled with the emotional derelicts that this sort of inattention produces.

Would that all those considering marriage and parenthood would take analytical looks at what their long-range goal options really are before "buying in." Best husband or wife material is not about the human equivalent of flashy wheels, pen-striped paint jobs, or mega-watt woofers and tweeters. Grand Champion children are not the product of 16 or 18 years of benign pasturing, climaxed by a single heart-to-heart corn feeding a week prior to graduation.

HOW HONEST IS HONEST?

If one accepts the validity of John Cortell's simplified child rearing formula, *"Be honest with them, and no baby-sitters"* (and I, for one, feel there is enormous value in this counsel), the question remains, *"How* honest?" or perhaps more precisely, "Are there instances where some deception is permissible?"

There is a certain security--even a cultural identity of sorts--rooted in some of our mythical traditions. We reckon with Santa Claus, the Easter Bunny, and the tooth fairy, until our children eventually grow into the awareness that that newspaper editor of yesteryear lied to Virginia, or at least was not totally accurate.

I wrestled with this dilemma before our first child was born. I wanted never to be guilty of deliberately misleading my child. Goodness knows I'm wrong often enough by accident without imparting information I *know* to be false. I feared that fostering the Santa Claus myth would eventually but inevitably call my credibility into question. Once my child or children determined that I given them false information about the above mentioned characters, they would feel justified in rejecting, or at least challenging other concepts and principles that I felt were important.

My wife felt that the excitement and mystery that surround these mythical characters justified our playing the game. So Santa came, as did the Easter Bunny, the tooth fairy, and (most generous, most mythical, and most real of all) Auntie Doris. Our youngest is now through college, so the mystique and secrecy surrounding the giving ritual is gone. And though I never directly *encouraged* my children in their childish misconceptions (while Renee did), their willingness to believe their mother over me today is at once amusing, touching, and mildly frustrating. My fears, it seems, were of shadows.

Still, I chafe at the attitude children sometimes develop that they are *entitled* by divine right to a new bunch of toys for no other reason than it is Christmas. I've seen this attitude manifested in people I've worked with, who seem to feel *entitled* to a paycheck for no other reason than they show up at the job site. I saw it where I worked with convicts who feel that the system and society they've preyed upon *owes* them access to law libraries and state funded lawyers to help them reduce sentences, and overturn justly imposed guilty verdicts on petty technicalities.

Ideally, children are loved, nurtured, and appreciated because they *exist,* whether or not it is Christmas, Easter, or their birthdays. And in the same ideal world they are taught to recognize that the society they live in owes them nothing beyond an environment conducive to the pursuit of productive and noble goals--or as the founding fathers put it, the _pursuit of happiness._ They are taught that wickedness never was happiness, neither can it be. They are taught that each gift has a price, and that *somebody* pays that price. They are taught that with every permission, every privilege, every license, comes a corresponding responsibility, obligation, or duty.

A gift tag reading, "To Johnny from Santa," seems to imply that there is a one-sided bene-"factory" somewhere near the North Pole that requires nothing from the recipient beyond sucking air. His diploma, his driver's license, his college degree, his paychecks will not be so easily obtained. We need an effective way of getting this idea across to him.

Gifts should be tokens of love and appreciation, values of which are understood by both the giver and the recipient. Thus, the giving ritual indulged in by Auntie Doris and the kids, and by the kids among themselves, is not merely still tolerated, but is more deeply valued and enjoyed now than ever.

Children should be indulged because they are loved, and because they *are*, and not simply because it is Christmas. Honestly.

ON LANGUAGE & CONCEPTS

One of the most exciting experiences of parenthood is witnessing a child's acquisition of verbal powers. From responding to words like, "bottle," "Mommy," and, "Bye-bye," progress is soon made to recognizing and identifying facial parts as they are named--nose, ear, eyes will be pointed to with glee as a child associates *sounds* with *things*.

Soon after, *concepts* begin to be understood. With ours (and with most children I've observed making the transition from gurgling to speaking) among the first concepts to be grasped are "No," and, "Mine." Children understand very early that "No" may mean anything from, "I'm not allowed to do that," to, "I don't want to take a bath," to "I can't have a cookie now," through an entire list of things forbidden to him--or things he does not intend to do.

But the concept of, *"Mine,"* and those relating to it, are delicate and sensitive issues, and parents should be aware that early impression on the young mind the nuances of what "mine" really means is one of the most important tasks of parenthood.

C.S. Lewis's Screwtape gives us a handle on it. *My* or *mine* can apply to anything from, "this shirt I can shred if I want," to "the woman who bore me," to "the employer who signs the paycheck." Obviously, the *"my"* of my shirt, my mother, or my boss does not mean the same in every instance. To the toddler-becoming-verbal, *"Mine!"* usually means, "Anything I happen to want." *Separating a child from this misconception can be frustrating for both parent and child, but it **must** be done, and the earlier the better.* Parents who neglect to correct this misconception when the process is still a simple matter do their children--and the neighbors and citizenry they annoy--no favor.

In any household there are many items that may be said to belong to the group--*our* soap, *our* table, or *our* backyard. Likewise, there are those things which Mom, Dad, and child have a legitimate right to call *mine* in the exclusive and most possessive sense of the word. That's Mom's lipstick, Dad's razor, and of course, that's Baby's toy.

With these concepts it must be taught that *our* bathtub should be left clean for the next bather; *our* milk should be returned to the refrigerator, and *our* dirty clothes should be the mutual responsibility of those who dirtied them. When they reach sufficient age and maturity, they can be taught to help with most chores. These concepts, if taught early, bear pleasing fruits as the children participate in class projects, take jobs, share dormitory rooms, and return home after extended absences.

If these concepts are *not* taught early, often children come to define, "my school" to mean, "the one I can litter with candy wrappers if I choose." "My car" means, "the one I use to terrorize random traffic and pedestrians with." "My radio" means, "the one I can play at 100 decibels wherever I want, and no one has the right to complain."

ON SYMPTOMS, DIAGNOSES, REMEDIES & IMMUNITY

The first step in effecting a *cure* for medical complaints is proper diagnosis. Diagnosis is critical because through it, we determine what *causes* discomfort, how to treat it, and how to avoid repetitions of the problem in the future.

During my years in the wood products industry, I suffered frequent and intense discomfort in my back and upper body joints. Diagnosis usually predictable--usually muscle strain or pinched nerves--but the *cause* was the nature of the work. Repeated attempts to move boards weighing several hundred pounds with one's body causes pain. When the pain becomes unmanageable, chiropractic realignment, medication, and rest are prescribed. All these help--temporarily--but the only *lasting* relief I ever got was when I quit manhandling boards that outweighed me.

In treating disease, sometimes *symptoms* must be treated prior to diagnosis. A fever of 105 degrees is life threatening, regardless of which microbe causes it, and it must be quickly checked. Once the fever is reduced and the germ identified, we turn to medical science for potions, pills, and powders to combat it. Ideally, preventive inoculations are given to those exposed or at risk to prevent recurrence.

What has this to do with parenting? *Most of successful parenting deals with a form of preventive medicine.* If doctors have as their goal the eradication of suffering, much of their effort will be in spent in vaccination administration. Parents who desire for their offspring contented, well-adjusted, productive and satisfying lives will take steps necessary to see that those children have learned behavioral hygiene, and have taken the inoculations, if you will, that improve the chances for achieving such lives.

Those children will have learned that fits and fevers of misbehavior will only be tolerated to a certain point before remedial action or quarantine is imposed. They will have been taught that pain resulting from over-exposure to sunlight is easier *prevented* than *salved*. So also with pain caused by exposure to alcohol, drugs, and association with germs. They will have been warned that some germs come in human form. They will understand that deadening pain with drugs does not remove the *cause* of the pain, and that this method of pain therapy is not a form of entertainment.

They will have learned that some pains and discomforts are therapeutic and curative, and although unpleasant upon administration, are calculated to prevent worse suffering down the road.

Not all medical treatment is oral, folks, nor will it ever be. Sometimes it involves traction, stitches, poultices, transfusions, and injections. It can even involve amputation. It is recommended procedure to inoculate children on their bottoms, not because we enjoy hearing them cry as hypodermic needles pierce their tender skins, but because we recognize that a minor puncture and a few days of muscle ache are preferable to bouts with debilitating diseases. The same principle applies for the administration of other forms of therapeutic discomfort.

In equipping children to become contented and contributing adults, preventive persuasions are preferable to corrective prison terms and psychiatric counseling sessions. The parent who thinks that persuasion can be accomplished with only sugar-coated pills and fruit-flavored tonics that go down painlessly, runs the risk of seeing his children ravaged by behavioral fevers that toddler-sized doses of mildly unpleasant vaccinations could have averted.

ON PIRATE DETECTION

The trading ships of yore were expected to fly the colors of their respective ports of origin. In port, they flew the colors of the port of call out of courtesy; on the high seas they flew the colors of their respective home nations. Lookouts in the crow's nests were able to identify other ships at great distance, and were thus able to determine whether they desired to communicate with one another. Perhaps dispatches were exchanged, or information concerning sailing conditions that lay behind the one and ahead of the other.

Pirates have been plaguing the legitimate merchants and traders for most of maritime history. In bygone days of sailing ships, the "Jolly Roger"--the dreaded skull and crossbones on a black background--came to symbolize pirates. Pirates would often use the ploy of flying false colors to lure potential victims close enough to attack, then run up the Jolly Roger and the battle was on.

The youth of practically every generation adopt standards of dress, grooming, and entertainment that give concern to their parents. The subject came up in our home on several occasions. Besides obvious reasons for parental protest (i.e. shorts not providing sufficient warmth for cold weather) there are several that give the young people fits. "Those baggy pants look ridiculous!" Or perhaps the clash in taste is over length or style of hair, or the length of an overcoat, or an offensive message emblazoned on a T-shirt.

Another element of concern has to do with "flying the colors." There are modes of dress, and even *items* of clothing or accessories that reflect the wearer's sympathies.

When we see a policeman's uniform, we have a right to expect that the person wearing it has been trained, and is committed to upholding and enforcing the law. We see an athlete in uniform, and we can tell which side he is on. The men and women wearing white in the corridors of hospitals we assume to be in the employ of the facility, and are there to render assistance to those with medical needs. In some cases improperly posing as an authorized wearer of a specific uniform is a punishable offense.

The movies and media have familiarized us with forms of pirates that inflict their predatory behavior on society. Some of these we readily identify by their modes of dress. We've seen pimps and drug dealers portrayed in gaudy, flashy clothes, driving exclusively expensive cars, carrying alligator-skin attaché cases containing samples of drugs, or pictures of girls in their "stables." We see outlaw bikers with their customized motorcycles, dressed in studded leather jackets, greasy denim pants, and heavy boots.

There is nothing inherently evil with fancy cars, or silk shirts and ties, or sharkskin suits, alligator attaché cases, or leather jackets. But those familiar with initiation rites for some outlaw motorcycle gangs, and knowledgeable about the symbolism of the colored feathers on the emblazoned eagle, know that no sensitive parent wants his or her child to be identified with that sort of pirate, and would not knowingly allow him or her to fly those colors.

When the mariners of yesteryear saw the Jolly Roger, they had a right to assume that they were in the presence of pirates. Because similar predators exist today, parents are justifiably concerned about the colors their children are flying.

FRUIT & FLOWERS; BULBS & BLOOMS

Portions of several summers of my teen years were spent laboring in the lily fields of Southwestern Oregon. The summer work consisted mainly of picking the blooms from the stalks and dropping them between the rows, to be plowed back into the soil. My last summer of high school I picked blooms for several different growers. When the harvest began in the fall, I worked for the father of a friend, and during this time I developed an appreciation for the process of raising lily bulbs to sell.

Those summers I spent picking blooms, nobody explained why the blooms were picked and left to rot back into the soil. It didn't really matter to me; I was paid to pick them and drop them, so I did. I mentioned to the grower during the harvest that it seemed an awful waste to throw the blooms away, since that was obviously the prettiest part of the plant. He said, "Selling lilies is not about *blooms*, Lad, it's about *bulbs*."

He explained the rationale behind picking the blooms. With no bloom on the stalk, nutrients otherwise expended to produce blossoms remain in the bulb, making it larger. The *bulb* is what the buyers are interested in. They replant the bulb in a greenhouse somewhere; the resulting plant and blooms from *that* planting are sold to Easter celebrants.

For the commercial grower, blooms are not desired *results*, but nuisances. All the planting, fertilizing, spraying, irrigating, weeding, and harvesting activities lily farmers engage in are calculated to produce not blooms, but *bulbs*.

Long after my exposure to the lily farming industry, I spent some time in fruit growing country. Cherries were the primary crop, though other fruits also did well in that area. One year we saw several weeks of exceptionally early spring weather, which naturally caused the fruit trees to bud out and bloom early. I discussed the situation with a grower, and offered the observation that he'd likely have a bumper crop that year. He was skeptical. "The problem with early spring is that the trees blossom early, then if the weather doesn't hold, and we get another freeze, it kills the blooms and we get NO crop." This turned out to be the case that year.

Fruit farming communities all over the country hold festivals, complete with ceremonies where Peach Queens and Cranberry Princesses are crowned, and paraded through town on elaborate floats festooned with blossoms of whatever fruit is being celebrated. We all admire the beauty of the flowers.

But it is worth remembering that the *money* crop for the grower is fruit or bulbs, and all the energy and resources they expend in the farming process is calculated to improve or increase the marketable product, however appealing to the eye the incidental beauty provided by his fields or orchards during the nurturing process.

Those who embark on a career of raising kids do well to consider at the outset what the desired end product really is, and select their farming techniques accordingly. Providing kids with designer jeans and $150 sport shoes admired by their peers is playing for the bloom. Buying them cars, complete with gas cards and insurance policies for their sixteenth birthdays is almost guaranteed to produce inferior fruit.

Children don't remain teenagers forever, any more than lily fields or cherry orchards remain constantly in bloom. Give them the care and treatment, the physical and emotional support and guidance that is calculated to produce well-adjusted, responsible adults--keeping in mind that such treatment might occasionally require the pruning or picking of a superfluous bloom and leaving it between the rows.

John Cortell's maxim sums it up: "Be honest with them, and no baby sitters." He didn't mean by that that a man and his wife should never attend a movie without the kids--but, he said, "We didn't take any week-long ski trips while the kids were growing up. We didn't even take any week-ends. If we couldn't take them, we didn't go." And his summarizing justification for his double-distilled, charcoal-filtered formula is worth citing again: *"If a child ever gets the idea into his head that there is something more important to you than he is, then you have no right to be disappointed when something becomes more important to that child than pleasing you."*

REACHING FOR TEACHERS

Given that parents cannot possibly teach their children *all* the things they need to know, how should they decide which teaching to delegate to others--and which other teachers to delegate it *to?* It is impractical, not to say impossible, to monitor and select every teacher, club advisor, coach, or scoutmaster your children will encounter through their growing years. Few will be of the first rank; many will fall below that elite status.

Trusting others with the academic, emotional, and spiritual instruction of our children is a chancy thing, and one that requires one of three attitudes:

(1) *A monumental leap of faith--a blind hope that those encountered will be competent, conscientious, and will have your child's interests as top priority, or*

(2) *A colossal indifference--a, "kicked-back, put 'em on autopilot" mentality that is almost guaranteed to bring grief, or*

(3) *A confidence in the preparation **we** have given our children in their first 5 or 6 years sufficient to quell the need for undue concern.*

If we have used bedtime stories, mealtime conversations, and Sabbath afternoons to maximum parenting advantage, our children will have encountered countless situations vicariously, through good stories and anecdotes from our own experiences. By the time they are ready for kindergarten they will have heard how others have dealt with danger, crises, and moral quandaries. They will have heard how unwise choices or poor decisions of some people brought pain and grief to those who made them--and to their loved ones. They will have seen that not all people are ideal, nor idealistic. And they will have begun to learn how to take the measure of the slothful, the incompetent, the predatory, and the ill-equipped.

By providing your children with the ability and *desire* to read (and *you* can do this as no other ever can!), and by making uplifting and inspiring material available, you can encourage them in directions and dimensions you hold to be desirable. By restricting and monitoring their television, movies, and other diversions, you can provide them with growth experiences that place a premium on hero selection, commitment to principle, and positive self-image. By discussing with them the biographies of real people, you can underscore elements you feel are important for them to understand and appreciate, and to cultivate these elements in their own characters. If your child hits the door of his kindergarten class already reading, and stoked about reading, it will take 3 or 4 dismally ill-prepared or incompetent teachers in a row to seriously retard his academic progress. He will read encyclopedias while his classmates are learning to tell b's from d's. I've been accused of being unrealistic--of being steeped in unproven theories--for making these claims. Eight honor students in a row have exonerated me.

We didn't do much worrying about which teachers our children wound up with as each school year began, although some of them did have preferences in given years. It was not because we were indifferent to their academic growth. It was because we felt confident enough in their preparation not to have felt threatened by the incompetence (or even merely the lack of stellar qualities) of a given teacher.

All of lasting value that *any* professional teacher can teach my children (that they can't learn in my own home) is *how to play someone else's game.* Make no mistake, this is an important concept for them *to* learn. It was my job (as it is your job to teach *yours*) to teach them how to recognize which games are worth playing.

WHICH GOAL, WHICH
TOOLS, AND WHEN?

The successful accomplishment of nearly every task involves the application of 3 basic principles. First, the goal should be clearly defined. Are we sweeping a floor, laundering clothes, or preparing children to function in the adult world? Second, the proper tools and materials should be assembled. Broom and dustpan, laundry supplies, and--Goodness! What all does one need in a child rearing tool chest? Third, of course, is some skill. Given that skills needed for successful functioning in the adult world are many, can we identify some as more important than others? Is there one that is *most* important?

Regardless of the interests and ultimate goals children opt to pursue, *reading skill* will be the key to achieving them. ***Reading is the key to all recorded human knowledge.*** The mind that has mastered the reading process is separated from *any* knowledge man has acquired only by his willingness and ability to visit a library. There he may find the requisite volume to bridge any knowledge gap, be it historical, scientific, political, or artistic. Reading is the skeleton key that unlocks any informational door.

So we taught ours to love reading, and we plead with you to do likewise.

Running close behind reading skills is the respect for the property, space, and sensitivities of others. The charm of many bright, well-informed and competent children is overshadowed by flippant, cynical, irreverent and smart-mouthed attitudes.

Children can be taught courtesy and manners as easily as they can be taught to tie their shoes, or to bathe themselves. It does require some focus--some periodic reminding of oneself and the student-child of the ultimate goal.

The vital nature of reading skills and respectful attitudes we couple with another truism: *That the **earlier** the child acquires these two essentials, the better off he is*. We were told more than once that sending our kids into kindergarten already literate made it rough on both the teachers and the kids, since the kindergarten curriculum was not designed for readers. The kids would become bored, restless, and prone to create behavior problems. That fear turned out to be unwarranted.

Each of our children heard me tell each teacher that we expected them to do well academically, for they were readers; that if they disrupted the class, we wanted to know about it *that day*, not at report card time, or even three days later by pink slip. They understood that there was *no* justification for annoying a teacher or classmate, and that there were many advantages to being co-operative and obedient.

If these skills and principles are not implanted early (during the pre-school years) it becomes increasingly difficult to implant them with each passing year. After age 10 or 12, it seems that an immunity to discipline develops, and sterner and sterner methods must be used to make the desired point, and with poorer and poorer success rates. Studies of rehabilitation programs show that persuading habitual miscreants to clean up their acts is *an exercise in futility once they have achieved adulthood*. If you doubt that, check on the recidivism percentages for convicted felons.

READING IS THE KEY

The success of your child in school, and in whatever he or she does following school, will be greatly dependent on his or her ability and willingness to read. As Mark Twain said, "The person who *won't* read has very little advantage over one who *can't.*" Listed below are ten maxims distilled from a program we developed, designed to teach parents how to teach their own pre-school children to read.

1. The problem of turning inquisitive youngsters into willing and competent readers lies at least as much in instilling a *desire* to read as in mechanical instruction.

2. The most crucial steps towards the production of readers are: A. Read to your children; B. Banish your television; C. Provide stimulating reading material.

3. Your child is capable of learning more, and at an earlier age, than most educators and child psychologists are willing to admit--and you are better able to teach--especially your own child.

4. ***Reading is the key to all recorded human knowledge***, and the earlier your child can read, the earlier he will encounter written bits of information that will enrich his existence. Reading is also the key to adventure, to humor, to music, or any other hobby. It is the key to *any* door he chooses to approach on any given trip to the library.

5. A willing reader will soak up more information accidentally, in his spare time, while entertaining himself, than the best teacher in the world can pound into the heads of his reluctant classmates using any conventional method.

6. Reading (learning) need not be a form of punishment.

7. **NEVER, NEVER UNSCREW THE LIGHTBULB ON A CHILD WHO IS READING!**

8. A picture is *not* worth a thousand words. The child that has mastered the reading process can encounter--vicariously--*any* experience that has been recorded in a language he understands. How much is *that* worth?

9. If your child graduates from high school unable to read, or reading poorly--after spending his first 5 years in your constant care, it will be *your* fault, and not the school system's.

10. You can make your child rich! Strickland Gillilan penned this little quatrain:

> You may have tangible wealth untold,
> Caskets of jewels, and coffers of gold.
> Richer than I, you can never be--
> I had a mother who read to me.

And we say:

> Yes, you can call it tangible wealth--
> My fortune is there, in the books on the shelf.
> And I'm richer than most, you'll surely concede,
> *FOR I HAD A MOTHER WHO TAUGHT ME TO READ!*

READING AS MOTIVATION & MOTIVATOR

If the entire body of written information existing in the world is seen as a treasure, then certainly *reading is the key* to that vault. Every single experience, idea, conjecture, or bit of reasoning recorded in the English language is mine--or yours--simply for the effort of going to a library somewhere and selecting the proper volume and reading it.

Why should you teach your child to read? Let us emphasize: Why should *YOU* teach *your* child to read? After all, don't we pay billions of dollars every year to fund education, and isn't the first of the "three R's" reading?

Most studies done on the subject of literacy in America indicate that 20%--that is *one in five*--of those who graduate from high school each June have difficulty reading a newspaper! The reasons for this are many and complex. But it is better to light candles than to curse the darkness, which is why we undertook the project of lighting our own little candles before we sent them off to school, and why we hope that you do likewise.

Schools are to the learning process what vitamin pills are to good health. Good health is not inherent in vitamin pills any more than learning is inherent in schools. Good health and learning occur in *individuals*. For those whose diets are inadequate, vitamins can contribute much to restoration and maintenance of good health. For the intellectually unmotivated (which includes most of us) schools constitute a supplement to our educational diets without which society would likely perish of academic malnutrition.

So we need schools. But a child given the ability to feed himself, and given a healthy appetite will gain more from a selection of academic groceries on the school/ supermarket shelf than one who will select voluntarily only those courses that are sugar-coated.

Virtually every child has a potentially vital and productive mind, just as every apple seed is capable of producing an apple tree. But a seed that is germinated under ideal conditions, sprouted in a fertile environment, fertilized, irrigated, weeded--when transplanted, will be in a better position to absorb nutrients from its new soil than a seed that falls neglected from a tree in a passed-over, half-rotten apple.

If you send your child into the school system already fired up about reading and learning, the result will be bushels and pecks of academic fruit where scrubby, poorly developed seconds might have been. I once firmly believed this as a *theory*. Eight growing seasons into the parenting game, I testify that this is *fact*.

The observation has been made that when you give a man a fish, you feed him for a day, but when you teach him *how* to fish, he can feed himself for a lifetime. Because of those complex problems existing in the education system mentioned earlier, it seems to us that the schools have given many of our children a fish or two. Some learn to catch a few. But the market is there for all they can ever hope to catch.

Don't send your child to sea with one fishing pole in a leaky boat! Give him the nets, fish-finding scopes, the steel-hulled, power-driven trawler that will make him the leader of the fishing fleet. ***Reading is the key***.

TERMS THEY UNDERSTAND

The most effective method of teaching children is to make learning worthwhile *in terms they understand*. In all the years we spent raising children I've seen much to support this position, and nothing to refute it.

Looking at techniques used by many educators, we see some that have become almost universal. The chief payoff for mastery of academic material is a grade, A down to F. These accumulate on the role book on assignments and quizzes for 9 weeks, then are tallied and averaged for the report card grade. Other related payoffs come as gold stars, smiley faces, or bonus points. Behavior is controlled through check marks, demerits, and loss of recess. These techniques are effective for many, but what about those who care nothing for A's, demerits, or gold stars?

Students receiving high grades and few checks on the "negative behavior" charts seldom view these things as ends in themselves. They learn, and behave properly because they have seen that there are other, more tangible benefits for doing so.

What was taught to our children as "acceptable behavior" we called "being nice." What the child behavior experts call "engaging in negative behavior," we called, "being naughty." And some of what those experts insist is "child abuse" we called "accepting the responsibility of teaching our children to mind." They did, and do.

We read to them, and taught them to enjoy a story for the sake of the story long before they were ever asked to memorize a list of main characters, or identify themes, plots, and symbolism. We helped them research topics in the encyclopedia long before they ever heard a teacher say, "Your assignment is…" Acquisition of knowledge became rewarding for its own sake, long before it was ever measured on the A to F scale.

One daughter read an encyclopedia from A to Z for a hundred dollars. A son continued piano lessons that had ceased to excite him for a ten-speed bicycle. Another conquered his fear of water and learned to swim for a hunting knife. These rewards were tailor-made for the children involved--prizes *they* understood and desired, and for which they were *willing* to produce. The money is long since spent; the bicycle long since stolen; the knife long since lost--but not the study habits, musical skill, nor the ability to swim. By the time report cards had become a factor in measuring the performance of our children, they had established such a history of success at mastering academic material that A's were not really needed to keep their attention focused.

They knew they were loved because they were *ours,* not because they got A's. We had explained to them that because of their number and our income, if college was among their goals, academic excellence would be of benefit to them, since scholarship and grant monies tend to be allotted to those who produce A's. This presented no new challenge, no need for revision of habits and outlooks. It simply called for a series of choices.

Individual interest is perhaps the most valuable motivational tool available to parents--or any other agent or agency, for that matter. Parents have the first shot at keying on it, exploiting it, of turning a child's *weakness* or attraction for something into a treasure chest of *strengths.* This applies to academic pursuits, as well as other areas less obvious and dramatic.

THE ROLE OF PUBLIC SCHOOLS

Achieving adulthood involves being able and willing to recognize the difference between an *opportunity* and a gift; the difference between a *tool* and its function; and the difference between a *recipe* and a finished cake.

Critics of the school system berate faculties and administrations because children reach a certain grade level not having mastered reading, or the times-table, or some other academic skill. The existence of a public school, and your child's attendance in it, will not automatically *guarantee* that your child will emerge from it "educated." A school cannot be compared with a cannery, in which a product (knowledge) is cooked, processed, portioned up, and sealed into student-sized cans. The school--the entire education process--is merely (and macroscopically!) an *opportunity*. The responsibility for capitalizing on it rests with the *students*, and *teaching* them--*encouraging* them--to capitalize on it *is the task of parents*.

Granted, there are some teachers who are more adept than others at wakening students to their potential--of "turning them on" to their opportunities. But the first--*best*--most likely place for this to happen--is in a home where Mom and Dad join in the exhilarating introduction to learning.

If children are not already excited about learning, their first assignments in school will be viewed as obstacles, as problems, as home**_work_**, with work in bold-face, italicized and underscored letters. Send them to school *already* reading, then encourage them in their learning tasks, and they'll never see learning as drudgery. Viewing schools as purveyors of a product called "knowledge," and criticizing them for not filling up our little "cans" is hardly fair, especially if we have not done our part in preparing the containers.

If you view the school as bearing the burden of pounding information into the heads of your children, you are not likely to be elated with the result. If you view the first 5 or 6 years of your child's life as an infringement on your career or your free time--if you *don't* see them as *priceless opportunities* to instill in them the love for good stories, for adventure, for discovery, for history, and for learning in general--then you have little right to be disappointed *with* or critical *of* a line-up of teachers who will be fortunate to achieve even mediocre success at the task.

School can no more be equated with educated students than a well-equipped and well-staffed dairy equates with quality milk products. The quality of those products is determined for the most part by what comes out of the cows--which is determined by what goes *into* the cows before they are led to the milking barn. If they have been into nettles and wild onions, all the high-tech equipment in the world cannot turn their milk into quality products. If they have been fed alfalfa, the cream content will be high, whoever milks them, and no matter what process is used.

The best schools in the world--and the worst--are merely opportunities. And while good ones may reach more students than poor ones, *the responsibility still rests on the individual student* to recognize and seize the opportunities before him.

Those who criticize the system's teachers for failing to prepare their children for college and the job market have to explain why others graduate from the same institutions literate, capable, and even with a term's worth of college credits behind them. All had the same opportunity to attend the same classes, and the option of choosing the same instructors, and of doing (or sloughing) the same assignments.

Not all mechanics with identical tool kits can perform the same quality of mechanical repairs. But the lack is in the *mechanics*, not the *tools*. May we teach our children early to view their schooling as a vast opportunity--as a *tool box*, rather than as some sort of finished "brain tune-up and overhaul."

SPORTS *OR* EDUCATION?

During my 5-year stint as a school board member, I was once asked a doubly disturbing question: "Why is it we can send kids all over the state playing ball, but can't give them a decent education?"

The first part disturbed me because I've been asking it myself for years in a more specific way: "Are we justified in spending *public monies* to fund inter-city athletic contests?" I have never heard a, "Yes, and here's why..." answer that convinced me. But either way, it is a question we are all going to need to re-examine carefully as education budgets tighten.

The second part disturbed me because on the one hand it was a foolish question, and on the other, it was the *wrong* question. No one can *give* any child an education. All we can hope to give him are *opportunities* to obtain one for himself. This we *can* do--and in fact *are* doing.

I had no knowledge of the academic records this man's children had amassed. But I had noticed during my time as a school board member that generally those most vocal in denouncing the quality of education their children were receiving were the least effective contributors to the education process, both as parents and as citizens.

Looking at the two parts of the question in juxtaposition casts light. Comparing the names on athletic team rosters to lists of scholarship recipients, we see many names that appear on both lists. Those who perform well in competition tend to perform well in the activity of mastering academic material. I'll not argue whether one causes or enhances the other. It is a moot point. The point is that athletic prowess and academic performance are not mutually exclusive; on the contrary, they seem to correlate. Of course, the correlation is not 1-to-1. (I had a state champion athlete once ask me how to spell "EACH"--and he wasn't kidding!) I've known honor students who have trouble bouncing a ball 6 times in succession, so mastery in one area does not *assure* success in the other.

All 8 of my children have now finished high school. One was an all-state caliber athlete, 3 were all-Northwest musicians; 3 were valedictorians (another finished second in her class with a 4.00+ g.p.a.); *all* were honor students, and most of them rode all over this end of the state (and two of them across the *nation*) to ball games, concerts, student council conventions, Boys'/Girls' State, scholarship interviews, and essay contests.

Which brings us to the last half of our question: "Why can't we seem to give them a decent education?" My response to this encapsulates my perception of what the *real* problem in education actually is--and it lies not within the walls of the institutions of learning, but in the *attitude* of too many of today's parents.

The whole concept of education has to do with the Latin root word, *e-ducere*, "to lead forth." You can't *lead* a creature if that creature won't move out of its tracks. The process of *educating* involves persuading, cajoling, bribing, inspiring, and instilling in the student the desire to *move forward with the learning process.*

Contrary to the belief of many, the job of doing that is not the *exclusive* province of professional faculties or coaching staffs. These can help, of course. They can hold out motivational carrots, and use all sorts of techniques to convey information--but unless the student *wants* to learn; *wants* to master new material; *wants* the freedom that acquisition of knowledge can provide--then the results of any educator's effort will likely be mediocre or worse--but not *ipso facto* the fault of the educator.

Motivating children to make the most of their educational opportunities is the job of *parents.* No one else has the personalized insight, the awareness of individual interests, tastes, preferences, and responses to a menu of stimuli that will inspire *my* child that I do. So how can I blame a teacher if, after an hour a day, 5 days a week for 9 weeks, he or she hasn't succeeded in pounding the multiplication table into my child's head?

It is a gross misplacement of blame to wait until an illiterate teenager has 13 to 18 years of lack-luster performance behind him, then criticize the school system for one's own lack of attention to the business of "leading his or her child forth."

The question my interrogator *should* have asked goes something like this: "What have *I* done wrong, that my child has spent 13 years in the same classrooms with your children--and yours can now read, write, compose and perform music, and can make change at cash registers--while mine can make nothing but smart-mouthed remarks and D-minuses?"

Wake up, Dilbert! It's not the sports program/education complex that has failed your child--it's *you*!

ON MEASURING & MOTIVATING

Among the frustrating weaknesses of the education process are the methods used first to *motivate* students, and second, to measure whatever progress those students might make. The same largely irrelevant emblem is used to both inspire and to gauge mastery--the big "A."

Nationally publicized instances of straight-A valedictorians presenting valedictory addresses in barely comprehensible English indicates need of better methods of measuring mastery, and more effective ways of encouraging students to attain it.

A co-worker complained to me once that his child had brought home a most unimpressive report card. Seeing a list of D's was the first inkling he'd had that his child was not learning! I thought, "How sad! Here is a parent who needs a paid professional--a mercenary tutor--to register his child's progress on the A to F scale every 9 weeks before it occurs to him that that child is sitting dead in the academic water."

There are other indicators much more reliable and much easier to monitor, which need no score keeping or tabulating by an extra-domestic agency. I would like to have asked some questions--ones any concerned and caring parent *can* answer about his own children, and which I could probably have answered for my friend's underachieving child without even asking. Among them:

How many hours had this child spent watching television during the last grading period? How many of those hours were prime time? How many books had he brought home from the library during the same period? How much time had he (the parent) spent talking with that child? How much of his free time was spent in wholesome, stimulating activities such as reading, creative hobbies, or mind-expanding games such as chess?

One does not need a scorekeeper with 9 weeks of assignment records to predict that a child who spends most of his uncommitted time skateboarding or boob-tubing is unlikely to dazzle anyone with his academic prowess. If the child in question is *yours*, and *you* can't answer these questions fairly accurately, it is not the teacher's fault that the grades were low, nor that you had no hint that they were going to be.

What if your child is one of those for whom A's stimulate no particular craving? Many parents resort to a pay-off schedule--five dollars for each A, three for each B, and a $50 bonus for straight A's. While it may be true that more kids will produce for money than for A's (and accompanying pats on the back), this is a dangerous tactic, and self-defeating for the parent genuinely interested in instilling the love of learning in his child. The *money* becomes the motivation; the A the means to it. And there are other--*easier*-- ways of achieving A's than mastering new material.

We rarely used prizes as incentives, and then only for clearly defined and tangible accomplishments. But I've always believed that the apparent ease with which our children learned was traceable *to* and measurable *by* their reading skills.

We began early to expose our children to the countless advantages of literacy--accessibility to stories, to information, to phone numbers, to merchandise in the super market aisles. When they began formal schooling they became immediately aware that literacy had several interrelated and highly desirable advantages--and that these would project as far into the future as their young minds could reckon.

They enjoyed the respect and envy of their classmates. They got preferential treatment from teachers. They felt no stress in dealing with home**work**. To them, learning had always been a series of *games*, and games are *play*, not work. They enjoyed security in their identities. They knew they were highly competent at their respective levels, and were justifiably confident of their ability to perform at the top end of the grading curve. By the time it occurred to them that there was anything challenging about new material, they had acquired a backlog of academic success, and an, "I can handle it," attitude. And a kid who *believes* he can handle it, *can* handle it.

They enjoyed being known as academic standouts, and preserving that reputation provided a far more attractive incentive than a new crop of $5-dollar bills every 9 weeks ever could have. Coupled with the inexpressible joy of learning--the innate pleasure--the almost spiritual enlargement of soul and consciousness that comes with acquisition of new knowledge--what other incentive is needed?

ON POWER OUTAGES

An anecdote appeared years ago in an issue of *"Country Woman"* magazine about a child who experienced the frustration of a power outage. The remote control would not make the TV come on. The manual switch was no help. Nintendo games would not show up. The child came to mother complaining in consternation, "Mommy, nothing works!"

Mom explained that yes, during power outages appliances run by electricity won't work, so for certain operations, we must improvise. The child retired to the bedroom for a few minutes, then returned with a hopeful question: "Mommy, do my story books still work?" YES!!!

A child *will be* entertained. If all one must do to accomplish this is to pull a switch and adopt a comatose posture before a lighted screen, that is what most of them will do. With that option *removed*, they will find *other methods*. They will nag someone to read to them. They will, believe it or not, read to themselves!

If parents have done their **home**work (heavy emphasis on HOME this time!), temporary power outages or picture tube problems, or even exiling the television to outer darkness--will not be perceived by their children as sentences to, "death by boredom." If you have read aloud to your children long enough to have ignited the love-of-a-story fire, power outages and rainy afternoons can be converted into excursions to Jack London's Arctic regions, Laura Ingalls Wilder's Little Houses, or Mark Twain's Mississippi River.

And if you have taken the time to introduce them not just to *story time*, but to *reading time*, you will have given them the most valuable tool, toy, information source, image enhancer, and entertainment center they will ever encounter.

We're not talking about a 2-year, hour-a-day, 5-day per week series of rote drills designed to familiarize a novice reader with 129 phonetic combinations in American English (or bore him to death in the attempt!). We're talking about 10 or 15 minutes here and there, as the child requests, or as you offer--making a *game* out of recognizing letters and numbers, and putting them together in different combinations.

If this is done in a loving, caring, non-competitive and stress-free environment, most children will sense that reading is a *friend*, not *homework*. They will see learning as fun and excitement--even more fun than muppets and more exciting than circuses. And by the time they encounter academically challenging material, they will be so far ahead of their classmates that they won't see new material as *obstacles*, but as *opportunities*.

I can't teach your kids to read like I did mine--but *you* can--if you will accept from the outset that it is *your* job, not some grade school teacher's; that they are *your* kids, not some pre-school's or Head Start program's; and that it is *your* kids' academic, social, and artistic careers that are important, not saddling the education system with blame for lackluster academic performances of your children.

Above all, you must recognize that if your child ever suffers from academic or social power outages, it is not the fault of the local school district/electric co-op, but that of the parents/electricians who designed his circuit panel.

MORE ON PIRACY

The captains of sailing vessels have always had problems to deal with that are unique to their trade--mutiny, piracy, uncharted shoals, and inclement weather to name a few. These perils (or forms of them) threaten other endeavors, but to ship captains they pose special dangers--ones that call for special skill and judgment.

In the era of wind-propelled ships, pirates were a constant threat. The captain of a merchant ship, after having safely piloted his ship to some distant port, and successfully bargained with the traders in his ports-of-call, and having skillfully kept his crew under control while outguessing the winds and currents, was always aware that there were pirates who would plunder his vessel, murder him and his crew, and scuttle his ship for the treasures acquired by his courage and skill.

Pirates used various tactics. Long John Silver, of *Treasure Island* fame, infiltrated and subverted the crew. This was not an uncommon method. Usually pirates would, by dint of superior strength and firepower, simply over power weaker vessels.

There was a particularly insidious form of piracy that used an especially cruel and indiscriminate method of preying on the unsuspecting and ill-prepared. They would place lights in places that would cause sailors to miscalculate the location of reefs and shoals; then when their ships ran aground, the scavenging pirates would be the first on the scene, invoking salvage laws to validate their claim to whatever booty they could gather.

* *

This voyage of parenting is different from those trading ventures of bygone eras in at least one important respect. The treasure IS the crew.

Jewels, spices, silk and gold--all these have market value regardless of their personal worth to the captain. He who was able to confiscate the contents of one or more of those ships could make himself and his pirate confederates wealthy beyond imagination.

The pirates that threatened my crew--and threaten yours--are generally easy to identify. Drug dealers care nothing for the inherent worth of their customers; they care only for their ability to pay in cold cash for the temporary high provided by drugs. Pimps and flesh merchants likewise care nothing for the girls in their "stables." Their only question is, "How much will other depraved men pay me for the use of their bodies?"

There are pirates in today's society whose motives are not easy to identify, but whose danger is every bit as real. There are those, who, for reasons known only to themselves, would mislead my crew members--who would teach them that there are no shoals, and that parents who try to teach them otherwise are old-fashioned, prudish, and puritanical.

"Sexual expression is natural," they say, "so go ahead--as long as you practice 'safe sex.'" They ignore the data that shows that since the days when "free love" was first widely advocated, teen-age dysfunction--to say nothing of STD incidence, unwed births, and suicide--have become epidemic.

There are those who would equate discipline with cruelty; who equate spanking with keelhauling; who would have the crew believe that the captain is, in fact, *not* in charge, and that they have legal right--or even obligation--to mutiny.

I find this sort of pirate more despicable than the thief. A thief I can understand, even if I cannot condone his thievery. But what does the subverter have to gain? How can he benefit from the mutiny, or even the poor performance of my crew?

Because I can't answer these questions, I am most fearful of their methods and tactics. I would warn all parents of the threat they represent. They should be required by the laws of the land and the laws of conscience to fly the Jolly Roger, for the poison they deal is as deadly as the cutlass in the hand of a buccaneer.

ON CROP FAILURE

Successful farming and ranching techniques have been developed over many centuries. People have long been aware that certain crops do best in certain climates; further, that by irrigating, weeding, and fertilizing, soil productivity can be greatly increased. It is axiomatic that the most successful growers are those who use techniques calculated to produce the best crops. The farmer who selects his fields with consideration to sun and wind conditions; who prepares his soil with proven tilling, fertilizing, and irrigation techniques, is *most apt* to reap the choicest crop.

Of course, he who systematically employs the best techniques still runs the risk of seeing his efforts destroyed by insect hordes or hailstorms. But over the long haul he will reap the rewards of conscientious effort, while his less industrious neighbors will cluck their tongues at his "good luck" and blame the inferiority of their own crops on anything *but* their own sloth or ineffective methods.

Crop failure, as a rule, is not the problem; it is the <u>symptom</u> of a problem. The problem is generally a combination of poor soil preparation, ignorance of vital factors such as soil chemistry, weather patterns, and lack of (or misfocused) effort.

Many communities are over-populated with parents who blame poor academic and social performances of their children on poor teachers, on poorly equipped schools, on apathetic administrations--and even on the fact that their children watch too much TV! (And whose fault could that possibly be?) There are those who trek to the principal's office to plead with administrators not to suspend or expel a child who has been "assaulted by bullies" for the 9th time in 2 months (when everyone in town knows that *their* child is the bully!); who complain when a child's report card sports a

C, three D's, and an F--and who claim they had "no indication" that the child was doing poorly until they saw the report card--whereupon they want the teacher fired.

Crop failure, as a rule, is not the problem; it is a <u>*symptom*</u> *of a problem. The problem is generally a combination of poor child preparation, ignorance of vital factors such as parent/child bonding chemistry, behavior patterns, and lack of (or misfocused) efforts.*

If you truly want your child to make the most of his educational opportunities, *prepare* him much the way successful farmers prepare their soil. Realize that all measurable success for 13 years will be metered by the child's ability and *willingness* to read. Show him that reading is his tool, his toy, and his friend.

Pull the plug on the TV long enough for him to recover from cartoon withdrawal. Expose him to the delights of the library. Acquire a shelf full of books, written at his level and somewhat beyond. Include a child's dictionary, and a set of encyclopedias (the first set need not be current, and they appear at garage sales for prices as low as ten cents on the dollar).

Teach him respect for teachers. Explain to him that while teachers are not always right, not always pleasant, not always compatible with your child's personality, they are always in charge, and are to be respected for that.

Teach him that there are people in this world who are hard to get along with--indeed, there are some who will not be gotten along with except on their own terms--and sometimes those terms are unacceptable. Teach him what his options are in those situations.

Teach him that the world operates on rules and laws, as do different facets of it; that rules are in place for good reasons; that changing them (or breaking them) entails risks that must be carefully examined before either of these courses is taken.

Teach him that broken rules bring consequences; that responsibility for disobedience cannot be passed on to another; that his right to be entertained ends at the point where it becomes annoying and/or dangerous to others. Teach him that *making the most of his educational opportunities is* <u>*his*</u> *responsibility.*

You should teach him these things because you realize some basic truths, among them:

(1) *That if he graduates from high school after 13 years of public school and 5 pre-school years in your home unprepared for the next phase of his life, YOU will have failed.*

(2) *That if he sits on the stand at graduation next to the valedictorian who has 11 advanced placement college credits, while he himself is functionally illiterate, there is someone to blame besides the remedial reading teacher, and that person sees the world through YOUR eyes.*

(3) **That crop failure (agricultural or domestic) is the <u>symptom</u> of a problem.**

*

I've been sailing parental waters now for over 40 years. As I make this entry, our baby has finished her bachelor's degree, so one might say the end of my voyage is in sight. I have learned much from exchanges with fellow sailors, and from the process of trial and error.

My desire to share some ideas and experiences with the community was encouraged by the local newspaper. My offerings as a columnist in a small town newspaper during the mid '90's were met with general acceptance, the only negative reactions coming from credentialed child behavior specialists. Their denunciation of my methods amazed me. I am a pragmatist. I wanted my children to behave in certain acceptable ways. We used methods calculated to instill this behavior. Voila! Our children behaved not only acceptably, they have behaved exceptionally--outstandingly!

We have heard from the school of Dr. Benjamin Spock and his followers. I look at a generation of children exposed to their methods and shudder. One need not read the logs and journals of many of today's parents to determine the success of their voyages--one needs only to look at the "cargo" they deliver. Say what you will about <u>our</u> methods; our cargo speaks for itself. To reiterate the statement made by Winston Churchill, "However beautiful the strategy, you should occasionally look at the results."

TO SPANK OR NOT TO SPANK

The following entry appeared as a column in the Curry Coastal Pilot (published in Brookings, Oregon) *in February of 1994. The following issue contained letters from 3 credentialed child behavior specialists who took vehement exception to the piece. I was accused of child abuse, advocating child abuse, ignoring relevant data, wasting books, failure to generate healthy self-images in our children, and of being lacking in patience, understanding, tolerance, kindness, and knowledge. The entry entitled,* "The Parable of the Soupmaker" *was prepared and submitted as a response to my critics. The editor refused to print it! I then prepared a lengthy diatribe which I felt successfully refuted their allegations. However, I spent too much time pontificating, and too little addressing the vital issue. Hopefully the version presented in the following pages will make the point more delicately.*

*

A much-debated topic among child behaviorists and parents is the question of corporal punishment. Critics of such methods usually use the argument, "If you spank a child you are simply communicating to him that it is okay for a bigger person to hit a smaller person in order to get one's way."

This argument misses the point. We have spanked our children. But I never hit a child because I am bigger than he or she is. When I spank a child it is because I am aware that my duty as a parent is to impress upon that child that certain behavior is not acceptable, and all other methods used to communicate this lesson have been unsuccessful.

If a child has no interest in respecting property rights, a new toy or a cookie might not provide sufficient motivation to establish that respect.

170

But everyone, young or old, understands discomfort. Certainly, you reason with a child, you explain to a child, and you persuade a child. But when these methods fail to produce the results you are after, the parent who refuses to use the tool of "applied psychology" is setting himself (and his child) up for some serious problems down the road.

One of our children developed an interest in dinosaurs bordering on obsession. Books were brought home on the subject which we learned had not been obtained in the manner described. Upon confrontation, confession was made. They had been stolen. "What happens now?" the culprit was asked.

"We better pay for them." Payment was made (out of allowance, several weeks in advance), apologies were made, then a fire was made in the fireplace, consisting of some pitchy kindling, dry wood, and the dinosaur book. We explained that while we were pleased at the interest in dinosaurs, we wanted to be understood that no book was valuable enough to justify stealing to obtain it. Then a bottom was warmed. My wife asked (in private, out of earshot of the kids) if I had been perhaps a bit harsh. I said, "I hope so. I want this to be the most traumatic experience of that child's young life."

A few weeks later Renee and the kids were enjoying an afternoon in the park when some older children stole a ball from our reformed dinosaur student, then ran to a house nearby. Renee knocked on the door and explained to the culprits that they should return the ball, or at least put it in the trashcan in the park with a newspaper over it, and that her husband would be there after work to retrieve it. If it was not in the can, he would come there after it.

Fortunately, the bluff worked. (With my luck, the kid's dad was probably an ex-SF 49er linebacker.) Upon retrieval of the ball, my child commented, "Dad, I learned something today. It's not much fun to have something stolen from you."

I hope the lesson is never forgotten.

*

THE PARABLE OF THE SOUPMAKER

Once there was a man who enjoyed making soup. He had not been trained in the culinary arts; had not attended the schools of famous chefs. His experience had been gained by tasting soups all over the world, and from discussing ingredients with cooks whose soups he admired. Basically, he followed the preferences of his own pallet. He knew what tasted good to him.

He had frequent occasion to serve guests in his home. Often soup was the fare. He frequently received compliments on the quality of his soups-- even from highly skilled cooks. He was even asked for recipes.

These requests became frequent enough that he decided it would be worthwhile to share his methods and ingredients with the community at large. He had no secrets--everything he had used or tried had been done by others.

He made arrangements to publish his soup making methods on a periodic basis in the local newspaper. One of his first contributions advocated the use of salt. The editor's page in the next issue was covered with outraged protests.

"Hasn't this man read the latest reports? Abuse of salt is bad for the system! Too much of that stuff will pucker your cheeks! And have you seen what happens when you pour salt on a slug? This man doesn't know about salt, and he doesn't know about cooking. It is dangerous to even let this idiot discuss soup making with an enlightened public! It is *chilling* to think of his ideas infecting and polluting the soups of an already improperly fed county!"

Understand, the man had never claimed that salt was the only ingredient in a good soup. He never claimed that it should always--or even ever--be the *first* condiment used. All he said was that sometimes it was called for, and when it was, nothing else would do.

And yet, for advocating the use of salt, the man's recipes were pronounced culinary travesties; he was labeled an imposter, and his soups pronounced unfit for human consumption--all by people who never tasted his soups!

ON SALT & SAVOR

In a discussion with my son, who was a few steps from completing his doctorate in Family Studies, I shared a pointed and caustic rebuttal I had written to the attacks from the child behavior experts. He chided me for being so defensive, pointing that both *they* and *I* had missed the salient points of my position. He said, "Dad, I feel the need to caution you about making such an issue of your use of 'salt.' How much 'salt,' percentage wise, did you use in the raising of us kids? If you feel the need to share your experiences with others, why not put emphasis on the *other* ingredients that make up the body of the soup? I can tell you as one of your children that the things I remember most about the way you and Mom brought us into line are certainly not the isolated and infrequent spankings (or doses of salt) I got--though I admit, many childish misbehaviors I *would have* engaged in, I decided to forego out of the desire to avoid another dose. [Consider the piece on Preventive Medicine!] What I remember most are the stories we read and discussed, the home evenings, the promises of rewards for good behavior, and the pats and praises for the same. Talk about *those* ingredients more, and salt less."

I reflected on this over the next few weeks and conceded that his counsel was good. I crunched some numbers. I recalled that the amount of chlorine required to purify a municipal water source is measured in parts per *million*. Surely the ratio of salt I used compared to other ingredients in the production of my "children soup" would rate comparatively.

I re-read some of my essays and columns on the subject, and was pleased to note that I *had* addressed in many of those essays the points he made, but I realized that they would present a more cohesive and methodical case if they were presented in a less random, more organized sequence to the inquiring parent. This volume is the result.

I conclude these ramblings with a summary that I feel addresses my frustration with the trends in child rearing, and with critics of my methods:

*

The Founding Fathers, in an audacious attempt to persuade the British Crown to recognize the colonies as free and independent states used the phrase, "We hold these truths to be self-evident..." The Declaration of Independence goes on to list some of those "self-evident truths," and no American since then has ever questioned or disputed in any way that there are, indeed, political truths that are self-evident. Self-evident truths are not restricted to those that apply to government and the way government deals with its subjects. Some of them apply to the rearing, nurturing, and preparation of youth to function as responsible adults.

I hold *this* truth to be self-evident: That too many of America's youth are being allowed to reach physical maturity without having learned basic concepts of duty, responsibility, respect for the rights and sensitivities of others, and respect for the laws and mores of society. The primary reason for this is *ineffective parenting techniques.* One of the most widely practiced of these ineffective techniques is our dumping of the responsibility of teaching these things onto the education system, or onto other mercenary institutions and organizations. And when these systems fail to do it--as they invariably must--we blame the systems!

Other self-evident truths are these: Children will do (1) those things that they *want* to do; (2) those things that they are *compelled* to do. The assignment of a true and worthy parent is to--step by cautious step--move those things that a child *ought* to do and those things he *must* do (whether because of physical necessity, or because of society's rules, or whatever) from the list of things he is *compelled* to do--across the page to the list of things he *wants* to do.

This assignment is accomplished over the years as the child learns that baths, bedtimes, the performance of chores, television off-switchings, and an entire list of other functions are *duties,* or *physical expedients,* or even survival techniques. The quickest and easiest way to get a child to exhibit a desired behavior is to make it pay off *in terms the child understands.* The wise parent uses persuasion, humor, bribes, threats, and as a last resort--force. If the former tactics are effectively employed, the application of the latter--the *ultimatum*--is a rarely used device. Thomas Fuller said, "Law cannot persuade where it cannot punish." I submit that this maxim applies to households as well as to political bodies.

Alexis de Toqueville, that articulate critic and observer of the young American republic, made the following comment--and although he was speaking in terms of nations and states, the principle applies just as certainly to families. Said he: "To render a people obedient and keep them so, savage laws inefficiently enforced are less effective than mild laws enforced by an efficient administration regularly, automatically, as it were, every day and on all alike."

Otega Y. Gasset said, "Civilization is nothing else but the attempt to reduce force to being the *last* resort." Paraphrasing Gasset, I would say, "*Effective parenting* is primarily the attempt to reduce force to being the last resort."

Just as the primary purpose of the law is not to punish, but to protect, the tactics and techniques of parents ought to be geared to the persuasion of their charges to perform as functioning, contributing citizens, rather than devising reasons to punish them, and ways of implementing that punishment. But for the vast majority of mankind, the *possibility* of punishment is a most effective motivator.

DEALING WITH BULLIES*

Most playground monitors and school principals believe (or have imposed on them) the doctrine that there is *never* sufficient justification for fighting. Those who have been abused, threatened, and pushed around by playground bullies in the absence of intervening adults know better.

My oldest son came to me after school one afternoon while he was in second grade. "Dad, will you teach me how to fight?" he asked. I explained that fighting was not the best way to settle one's differences. He responded, "I know that, Dad, but there's this kid..." Then followed the litany that describes the typical playground bully most of us have encountered at some time in our lives.

I had managed to reach this point in my life with a fairly limited number of fights, but the few I lost made me wish I had been better prepared. I agreed to teach him what little I knew. I got him a pair of lightweight boxing gloves. I showed him how to hit straight from the shoulder and how to penetrate the "windmill" offense often seen in playground squabbles. He learned quickly, and after the fourth or fifth lesson, left me with a puffy lip.

"Okay, that's about all the physics of self-defense I know," I told him. "Now, a point or two of theory and philosophy. First, you don't owe a kid a fight just because he wants one. It's generally best of avoid a fight if you can. But if you can't negotiate your way out of one without sacrificing unacceptable quantities of face, property, and dignity, then you hit first, hard, and often, until they drag you into the principal's office. Second, most kids believe they are dying if they see their own blood. The only place *you* can draw blood with your fist is *face, dead center.* Noses and lips bleed easily. So your first blow should be targeted, bull's eye *NOSE.* Third, they are wrong about equating bleeding with dying. No one ever bled to death from a bloody nose or a split lip. If it is *your* lip that is dripping blood, and you keep coming at him, he'll think he's fighting a dragon, and will likely quit. Got all that?" He said he did.

"Now, last, and most important for you to remember. If you absolutely feel you *must* fight, then use what I've taught you, and when they take you to the principal's office, call me. Likely you'll be suspended or expelled, but if I'm satisfied that you were justified, it's okay. If you are wrong--and believe me, I'll find out--if you've thumped some kid's melon because he combs his hair funny, or his clothes are out of fashion, or his sister is ugly, or his skin is a different color, or any of that nonsense--then whatever else the school does to you, you'll still have me to deal with, and it will be many years before you can handle me. Do you understand what I've just said?" He did.

Second grade passed, and third. Well into fourth grade he announced to his Mom one day that he had flattened the bully. I expected a call, but it never came. At conference time I asked his teacher about it. "Ah, yes--I'm not sure of the particulars, but I've been watching it coming for a couple of years. The boy your son hit likes to push, and has been pushing for a long time. Evidently your boy got tired of backing up. I heard kids yelling, 'Fight!' and looked over at Jonny laying on his back with Loren standing over him, with fist drawn back. I've learned over my years on the playground that sometimes it's not a bad idea to let the kids get in a lick or two before intervening, especially if the one who 'has it coming' is getting it. I slowly started across the playground, and the bell rang. The kids all ran in under the shelter--all except Johnny, who waited until Loren was well out of range."

Understand, I'm not recommending that every parent enroll his or her child in a martial arts class, nor am I criticizing the schools for holding to a "no excuse" policy towards playground altercations. It is neither my desire nor intent to determine policy for the entire world. All I hoped to do was to equip my children to deal with that world. And no one in recorded history has ever successfully negotiated with a bully from a position of weakness.

*This piece was written as a column, but never ran. The flap over the "To Spank or Not to Spank" offering prompted me to do the revision that follows— which obviously never ran, either.

DEALING WITH BULLIES REVISED*

My oldest son came to me one day while he was in second grade. "Dad, will you teach me how to fight?" he asked.

"Son, fighting is not the best way to settle your differences," I replied.

I know that, Dad, but there's this kid..." Then followed the litany that describes the playground bully most of us have encountered at some point in our growing up.*

"An ideal world is free of violence, Son. If we really want this to be an ideal world, we must never be guilty of contributing to the violence that is in it. We do want peace, don't we?"

"Well, yes, but..."

"Hitting back is contributing to violence, so here's what we'll do. We'll get you a pair of track shoes. We'll go up to the track three or four nights a week and we'll run wind sprints. We'll practice until you have the school record in the 400 meter run."

"Why the 400, Dad?

"It's called a 'cushion,' Son. As long as you are on school property, you'll never be more than a couple of hundred yards from a teacher or playground monitor to hide behind. When a bully becomes too menacing, just outrun him to the nearest adult, who will protect you, okay?"

"What if I can't outrun him, or there's more than one?" he wondered.

"That's a tough one, Son. There are a couple of things you can try. First, of course, use the reasoning approach. Explain that hitting makes guidance counselors and child behaviorists very unhappy, besides making you uncomfortable."

"And if he won't stop, what then?"

*Anyone who really believes this conversation went as described from the asterisk down, I have a banana plantation in the Klondike I'd like to sell you. Anyone who believes it **should** have gone like--pray daily that the bullies all become converted to the "never okay to hit" philosophy before your child is forced to deal with one.

"Well, you can always hope that the sight of blood will make him squeamish. Try to maneuver your face in front of his left jab. Noses and lips bleed easily. If the sight of your blood doesn't discourage him, bleed on his high-dollar Air-Bully running shoes.

"Don't worry if he breaks a couple of your teeth. We have dental insurance."

"That's it? That's how I'm expected to deal with bullies?" he asked, incredulously.

"Only until you're out of high school," I answered. "After that, I recommend you move close to a police station, and get a cell phone and memorize 911 and other emergency numbers. You may get lucky and never encounter a bully after high school. I haven't had to deal with one in years."

"Boy--8 years of school left, and I have to be able to outrun every bully in town? I don't know, Dad..."

"Listen, Son--we've got a whole battery of well-schooled and highly qualified guidance counselors in this end of the county hard at work right now teaching people that it's 'never okay to hit.' Who knows? Maybe by the time you're in high school there won't be a bully left in town. And just think of the condition you'll be in! You'll be brim full of confidence, self-esteem, and all those good things--you may even be an all-state sprinter. And you'll owe it all to doing your part in maintaining world peace. If you are still uncomfortable with this plan, perhaps we could get you a whistle and a can of Mace. Anyway, since what we really want is peace, we can always hope for a best-case scenario. Maybe you'll never meet another bully. But *if* you do, and by some miracle you become the first in the history of the world to successfully negotiate a peace from a position of weakness, think of the glory you'll get. Trust me, Son--it's never okay to hit."

* * *

Thus endeth this chronicle. "When one writes about grown people, he knows when to stop--that is, with a marriage," wrote Mark Twain, "but when he writes of juveniles, he must stop where best he can."

The story of parenthood begins with a marriage, or certainly ought to. But when does it end? Does it ever end? This voyage began for me in 1972 with the birth of our first son, though I hope it is clear that preparations for it began much earlier. Our youngest daughter has completed her bachelor's degree at this entry, and has recently wed, so I suppose one could say that the harbor is on the horizon.

Children cease to be children; they never cease to be sons and daughters. Children become parents, and eventually the progeny that makes them parents become parents in turn.

So where does the voyage end? When the last crew member leaves the ship? Perhaps we gain emeritus voyager status, and begin a treatise on grandparenthood.

If my crew or any fellow sailor has been enlightened or entertained by these musings, I am pleased. Just as those early seafarers benefited from exchanges of nautical information, so we can gain from sharing information on the methods we have used to avoid and to cope with the hazards that threaten our voyages. I, for one, appreciate all the help I have had.

Again, good luck, and good sailing!

AUTHOR INFORMATION & CREDENTIALS

James Lawrence Marks
Born: December 14, 1943 in Albany, Linn County, Oregon
Education: High school – Brookings Harbor High School, Brookings, Oregon, 1962
  College: Bachelor of Arts in English, University of Utah 1973
Married: Renee Fluckiger, of Bedford, Wyoming August 27, 1971
Children: Loren Dean, Heidi, Holly, Jamie, Jeremy Lawrence, Jill, Jacki, and Doris

To date (February, 2017) all have graduated from high school with an amassed grade point average of 3.875.

Loren got his Bachelor's and Master's degrees from Brigham Young University, following a two-year mission for his church in Wisconsin. His doctorate is from the University of Delaware. He was a professor at Louisiana State University in Baton Rouge, Louisiana until 2015, when he moved to BYU. He and his wife have 5 children.

Heidi obtained her Bachelor's degree in 3 years and Master's in 4 at Oregon State University, and taught high school English and Spanish at Hidden Valley High School in Murphy, Oregon, until 2015. Heidi is married, and they have four children.

Holly has her Bachelor's degree from Western Oregon University in Monmouth, Oregon, and worked for several years in the computer technology industry. She is married with 4 children. She has taught piano and voice, and is organist for her local Church unit.

Jamie completed a year of nursing courses, then married her high school sweetheart. She hopes eventually to obtain a nursing credential and return to the work force. She served as chairperson for her local school board. She has 4 children.

Jeremy completed one year of undergraduate studies at Western Oregon, then served a 2-year mission for his church in Louisiana. He is currently employed as a correctional officer at Pelican Bay State Prison in Crescent City, California. He and his wife have 6 children.

Jill has a Bachelor's degree from Brigham Young University, and is currently working in Washington, D.C. She is single.

Jacki completed a year of nursing courses before marrying. She and her husband have three children, and are living in Orem, Utah.

Doris has her Bachelor's degree from Brigham Young University, and is married. She and her husband have 2 children.

Four (Heidi, Holly, Jacki, and Doris) all had 4.00 or better grade point averages in high school. Besides academic accolades, these 8 children amassed drawers full of awards for music, athletics, and student leadership. Three (Heidi, Holly, and Jill) skipped grades. Their honor student status was earned against the most intense academic courses available, including calculus, physics, and Advanced Placement classes in several subjects. In the 101 student years they attended public schools, we never once were called in to bail them out of the detention room or the vice-principal's office for misbehavior. They were good kids.

THEY are our credentials.

APPENDIX

(The data listed below is taken from a report entitled "Louisiana Governor's Program on Abstinence, pages 34 and 35.)

HEALTH CRISIS INFORMATION

In 1970 there were two major sexually transmitted diseases (STD's). Today there are 25 major STD's.[1]

The U.S. population in 1970 was 205 million.[2] The number of STD's reported to public health was 692,870,[3] or one out of every 300 Americans. The STD's were bacterial and curable.

The U.S. population in 2000 was 275 million (see census report listed above). 70 million Americans had a viral, incurable, STD – 45 million with herpes[4] and 25 million with HPV[5] –or one out every four Americans.

The term "safe sex" first appeared in America in the 1980's in an attempt to alleviate the wide spread fear of AIDS.[6]

---

[1] Thomas R. Eng and William T. Butler "The Hidden Epidemic – Confronting Sexually Transmitted Disease" Washington D.C. National Academy Press 1997

[2] U.S. Census Bureau, Statistical Abstract of the U.S. 2000 No. 2 Population 1980-2000

[3] Centers for Disease Control and Prevention. Summary of Notifiable Diseases, United States, 1997, Morbidity and Morality Weekly Report; 46 (53) Atlanta, Georgia.

[4] "STD's in America: How many Cases and at What Cost?" 1998, Menlo Park, Calif. Kaiser Family Foundation and American Social Health Association.

[5] Center for Disease Control and Prevention. MMWR Surveillance Summaries. June 28, 2002/51 (sso4) 1-64.

[6] "Safe Sex" – sexual activity in which precautions are taken to ensure that the risk of spreading sexually transmitted diseases (especially AIDS) is minimized. The Oxford Dictionary of New Words Oxford New York, 1997 Oxford University Press.

The estimated number of new cases each year for the four leading STD's are: HPV (5.5 million); Trichomoniasis (5 million); Chlamydia (3 million); and Genital Herpes (1 million). (see footnote 4)

For every unwed teenager who gets pregnant this year, 10 teenagers will become infected with an STD.[7]

There is NO clinical proof that condoms or other contraceptives prevent HPV, Trichomoniasis, Chlamydia, or Genital Herpes.[8]

One in ten teenage girls has Chlamydia.[9]

Nearly 50% of African-American teenagers have Genital Herpes.[10]

85% of people with Genital Herpes have no clinical signs of infection.[11]

Today the most prevalent STD is the Human Papilloma Virus (HPV) There will be 5.5 million new cases of HPV in America this year. (see footnote 4)

HPV can be spread by skin-to-skin contact, and does NOT require that an act of intercourse take place to be transmitted. Condoms cannot protect against infection with HPV.[12]

99.7% of all cervical cancer worldwide is caused by HPV.[13] 5,000 American women will die this year from cervical cancer. (See footnote 1) Most cases of cervical cancer occur in women before the age of 25.[14]

---

7   Centers for Disease Control and Prevention, National Center for Health Statistics. National Vital Statistics Report, Vol. 48 No. 18 Hyattsville, Md. 1999

8   National Institute of Allergy and Infectious Diseases, National Institutes of Health, Department of Health and Human Services. Workshop Summary: Scientific Evidence on Condom Effectiveness for Sexually Transmitted Disease (STD) Prevention July 20, 2001.

9   National Center for HIV, STD, and TB Prevention, Centers for Disease Control, U.S. Department of Health and Human Services. "Tracking the Hidden Epidemics." http://www.cdc.gov.2000.

10   D.T. Fleming et al. "Herpes Simplex Virus Type 2 in the United States, 1976 to 1994" New England Journal of Medicine 337 (1997) 1105-1160.

11   Lawrence Cory and H. Hunter Handsfiled, "Genital Herpes and Public Health" Journal of the American Medical Association 283 (2000) 7-33.

12   American Cancer Society Cancer Facts & Figures 2000

13   Journal of Pathology 189 12-19 (1999)

14   Robert Greenlee, Taylor Murray, Sherry Bolden, and Phyllis A Wingo, "Cancer Statistics 2000" Ca: A Cancer Journal for Clinicians 50 (2000): 7-33

More women die each year from HPV/cervical cancer than from HIV/
AIDS. (See footnote 8)

The number of high school students that have engaged in sex has
decreased by 15% since 1990. (see footnote 5)

For every dollar spent on STD prevention, $43 are spent on treatment.[15]

Sexually transmitted HIV represents just 0.13% (20,000) of all
projected annual cases (15.3 million) of STD's. (See footnotes 4 and 8)

In 2001, 22,5% of white births, 68.6% of black births, and 42.5% of
Hispanic births were out of wedlock.[16]

---

[15] "Confronting a Hidden Epidemic: The Institute of Medicine's Report on
Sexually transmitted Diseases: Family Planning Perspective, Alan Guttmacher
Institute, March/April 1997

[16] National Center for Health Statistics, Centers for Disease Control, U.S.
Department of Health and Human Services. "Births: Final Data for 2001"
http://www.cdc.gov/nchs/releases/02news/precare.htm

Printed in the United States
By Bookmasters